Teaching Social Behaviour

Classroom Activities to Foster
Children's Interpersonal Awareness

David Warden and Donald Christie

David Fulton Publishers
London

David Fulton Publishers Ltd
Ormond House, 26–27 Boswell Street, London WC1N 3JD

First published in Great Britain by David Fulton Publishers 1997

Note: The right of David Warden and Donald Christie to be identified as the authors of this work has been asserted by them in accordance with the Copyright, Designs and Patents Act 1988.

Copyright © David Warden and Donald Christie 1997

British Library Cataloguing in Publication Data
A catalogue record for this book is available from the British Library

ISBN 1–85346–469–4

Typeset by Textype Typesetters, Cambridge
Printed in Great Britain by Bell and Bain Ltd, Glasgow

Contents

Acknowledgements

The research reported in Chapters 3 and 4 was part of a larger project jointly funded by the Mental Health Foundation (Scotland), the Scottish Office Education Department, and the University of Strathclyde. The data reported in these chapters was gathered by Claire Kerr and Jenny Low. The cartoons shown in this book were all drawn by Craig Stevens.

Chapter 1

The Social Development of the Child

There is widespread and growing concern, in educational circles and beyond, at the apparent rise in antisocial behaviour among children, ranging from discipline problems in the classroom and the increased incidence of bullying, to a more general lack of respect for others, in terms of their feelings, person and property, and occasional and notorious cases of violent crimes involving children. Such problems co-exist with wider social changes, including, regrettably, increased inequality, family breakdown and a weakening of parental control, unemployment, various forms of physical and sexual abuse, and a significant youth crime and drug culture. While these negative influences need not lead to behaviour problems, neither do they provide a satisfactory climate for the socialisation of children, a process which is of crucial importance to families, schools and society.

This book is about the development of children's social behaviour, about their abilities to engage in social interactions and to form social relationships. More specifically, it is about the development of good and bad, or prosocial and antisocial behaviours. Our aim is to contribute to children's social education by providing teachers with a set of classroom tasks and activities which will foster children's prosocial behaviour by encouraging them, on a regular basis, to discuss interpersonal feelings and behaviours, and to consider the feelings and points of view of other children.

This first chapter provides a psychological perspective, with a discussion of the skills involved in forming social relationships, such as empathy and communication skills, and their development. Children's social behaviour is also affected by their understanding of the difference between right and wrong, and of the social and moral rules which guide our interactions with each other, and we shall examine how such understanding develops and changes. In Chapter 2, we turn our attention to the current educational perspective, and its growing emphasis within the curriculum on personal and social development. In Chapters 3 and 4, we consider whether we can assume consensus on what constitutes 'good' and 'bad' social behaviour, or whether these

Introduction

are shifting categories, subject to different peer group and sub-cultural definitions. The second half of the book, Chapters 5 to 8, is devoted to a presentation of the materials and procedures to be used and adapted in classroom activities. Most of these tasks will involve peer interaction, and the intention is that, by incorporating such interpersonal activities into the school curriculum, it will help children to achieve a more consensual and cooperative approach to social relationships.

Let us begin by considering psychological theories and research which are relevant to the development of children's social interaction skills and interpersonal relations, and to their understanding of morality and the rules of social behaviour. In discussing psychological theories, it is important to remember that, while they are strongly rooted in empirical research, they can only provide a general framework within which to interpret the social behaviour of the children in our care. We also need to be aware of those societal changes which may influence the nature of family life, and of children's intra- and extra-familial interactions, and hence the nature of their socialisation. For example, growing parental fears about their children's safety can have a constraining effect upon the freedom and variety of children's leisure activities and hence their opportunities for social interaction. An increased reliance on television and computers as leisure-time activities may also have an influence upon the nature and development of children's social skills. We must also remember that individual children are subject to an individual set of circumstances, possibly including family instability, social disadvantage or some form of child abuse, which will impinge upon their understanding of social and personal relationships, their moral sensibilities and emotional needs, and consequently upon their social behaviour. The challenge is to be able to take account of such circumstances in our responses to their behaviours.

Social intelligence and understanding

Participation in social relationships requires a form of intelligence which has often been ignored by intelligence tests, with their traditional focus on the more obviously cognitive and educational elements of intellectual processes. However, more recent theories of intelligence rightly acknowledge the importance of social intelligence, that is, an awareness of self and of others, and the ability to interact and to communicate with other people, and to have some understanding of their mental states. Indeed, an essential prerequisite for social interaction is the ability to distinguish between one's own thoughts and feelings, and those of others; social partners must not only acknowledge each other as separate individuals having different perspectives on the world, but also be able, to a certain extent, to predict, interpret and respond to each other's different beliefs, desires and intentions. For example, if you lose something important to you, I can predict that you will feel upset; if I know that you believe something to be true, I can predict that you will be surprised if you learn that it is false. In other words, on the basis of what I know about your expectations and past experiences, I can impute something about your mental state, and choose to act accordingly.

What do we know about children's developing awareness of the mental states of others? The work of the Swiss psychologist Piaget on the egocentricity of children's thinking and understanding has tended to dominate this question. Based on a series of classic experiments, such as the three mountains task, his theories suggested a process in which children's thinking gradually becomes socialised around seven years of age; but that, prior to that age, children have considerable difficulty in being aware of any perspective on the world but their own. However, having some difficulty does not mean that they cannot do it at all, and more recently, researchers have examined the early beginnings of children's understanding of the mental states of others, or the development of children's 'theory of mind', as this research topic has come to be known. When do children begin to explain and predict other people's behaviour and emotions in terms of their mental states, for example, their beliefs and desires? And how does the development of such mind-reading ability affect children's capacity for social interaction?

One of the tasks used to examine children's theory of mind is the 'false-belief' task. In a typical version of this task, the child being tested is presented with a scenario in which one character, John, wishes to retrieve something which he has previously placed in location A, but which, in his absence and unbeknownst to him, his brother Colin has moved to location B. The child whose theory of mind is being tested has witnessed John's initial deposit and Colin's subsequent removal; she is then asked to predict where John, on his return, will look for the item – either in the place where John put it and still thinks it is (location A), or where she as observer knows it now is (location B). Generally speaking, three-year-olds fail on this type of task, predicting that John will look in location B. Four-year-olds are more successful: they can recognise John's false belief and predict that he will act upon it by looking unsuccessfully in location A. What is interesting is that research is beginning to seek and to find correlations between children's performance on such tasks and certain aspects of their social behaviour, especially their communication style, and their emotional understanding. For example, when they engage in pretend play, children are sharing an imaginary world; they must, therefore, be able to make their own imaginary worlds explicit so that others can participate. Between the ages of three and five years, children's increasing success on false-belief tasks is significantly associated with the extent to which, when at play, they do explicitly communicate their own version of this pretend world to their partners. Young children's competence in these tasks also seems to be linked to the extent to which family, especially mother–child, discussions have typically focused on feeling states and causal relations. Again, the better 'mindreaders' appear to be more aware of, and sensitive to the judgements and criticisms of others. There are also indications that the development of a moral sense depends upon an understanding of the emotional states of others.

The ability to predict and interpret other people's mental states is a considerable advantage in social interaction. It allows us to empathise and share their feelings, which is central to the development of friendship; it allows us to surprise or amuse them by contradicting their expectations; and it allows us a degree of control over their behaviour. If I know something of what you know or expect, or conversely, if I know what you don't know, I can use this knowledge to my own advantage. The desire to control or manipulate other people's behaviour or their mental states appears early, as any parent will confirm. By eighteen months or earlier, a rudimentary form of child-initiated teasing can be seen in many parent–child interactions, which is clearly designed to elicit parental reaction. For example, a son of one of the authors (DW) used to pretend he was going to put his fingers in electric power sockets, and be highly amused at the panic reaction he achieved.

Teasing, pretence, deception and the keeping or sharing of secrets are all forms of social behaviour which depend to a more or less explicit degree on an awareness of the different mental states of the participants. In games of teasing and pretence, young children learn to represent false realities, they play at making others believe something that is not true. But there is a complicity in such mischievous misrepresentations of reality, or of mental states, whereas, when they graduate to the duplicity of telling lies, children are deliberately trying to maintain a difference between their own and their listener's knowledge. Keeping a secret may necessitate telling a lie, but it also involves a social contract between two people who share a mental state, and who agree to exclude others from it. Children's understanding of and feelings about a secrecy contract and its imposition – its motives, and the consequences of breaking it, will depend on their ability to interpret and predict the mental states of the other parties to the contract. While five- or six-year-olds may enjoy the responsibility of keeping a secret, ten-year-olds are more likely to feel uneasy about the consequences, for themselves or others, of either keeping or divulging the secret. Indeed, secrecy places strains on children's mind-reading capacity well into early adolescence, and this has further implications, in the context of abuse prevention, for children's ability to differentiate between a good and a bad secret, which importantly entails moral decision making. However, these aspects of social awareness would appear to be amenable to change and development in the context of relevant experiences, planned or otherwise (Dunn 1993). The educational justification for increased provision of such experiences will be discussed in Chapter 2.

Empathy and role-taking

Empathy is a form of emotional mind-reading which has particular significance within personal relationships; being empathic means having 'an affective response more appropriate to someone else's situation than to one's own' (Hoffman 1987). Thus we can empathise with a friend whose spouse has died, who is in financial distress, or who has won the lottery; we can also empathise, often via the media, with the victims of poverty, war or criminal action. Even two-year-olds can demonstrate a form of empathy, insofar as they can become distressed at another child's distress. However, this has been termed 'egocentric empathy', because the child so aroused is deemed unable to understand what has caused the other's emotion, or what might alleviate it. The developmental course of empathy requires (a) an awareness of the separateness of other people as individuals (by two years), (b) an awareness of the mental state of others, and that their feelings in a situation may differ from one's own (developing slowly from three years onwards), and (c) an awareness of others' different attitudes and life experiences and the ability to interpret their feelings in the light of such knowledge (gradually from late childhood onwards).

There is also a constructive element to empathy which goes beyond vicariously experiencing another's emotion; empathising can also produce feelings of sympathetic concern for the victim and a conscious desire to help; in this sense, the role of empathy in the development of prosocial behaviour becomes clear. There is growing evidence of an association between empathic ability and prosocial behaviour in children: the more a child is sensitive to the feelings of others, the more likely she will be to exhibit helping or sharing behaviour when it is needed. Relatively stable individual differences in the level of children's empathic responding have also been noted, in children aged between two and seven years. Like adults, young children may respond to another's distress in different ways – by expressing distress themselves, by avoidance of the distressed person, by being angry and aggressive, or by expressing an unemotional, analytical interest in the reasons for the distress. It has been argued (e.g. Barnett 1987) that the roots of such individual differences lie in children's different socialisation experiences, for example, levels of parental affection, whether a child is encouraged to consider the feelings and emotions of others within the family, discussions of feeling states, etc.

The development of children's role-taking ability has been most famously, if controversially, described by Robert Selman (1980), who proposed a five-stage model of social perspective taking from the age of 4 to 15 years and beyond. In the first stage (4–6 years), the child is largely unaware of differing perspectives to her own ('there is only my perspective and I assume you share it'). Gradually (stage 2, 6–8 years), she realises that others have different (but wrong) perspectives ('there is only my perspective, I realise that you don't understand it yet, but I'll help you to understand'). Between 8 and 10 years (stage 3), children grasp the reality of differing perspectives, and begin to see their own behaviour from another's perspective, and to achieve Robert Burns' desire – 'tae see oorselves as ithers see us'. Around 10–12 years (stage 4), the beginnings of mutual role-taking and a metaperspective appear ('I know what you think, and I know that you know what I think'). Obviously at this level, considerable role-taking and mind-reading skill is required, and the final stage (12–15 years and beyond), in which the adolescent child demonstrates a growing awareness of the complexities and subjectivity of social perspectives, may not appear at all.

At this point, the reader may be a little confused by a discussion which has considered the development of three nominally different but clearly overlapping children's abilities, namely, to interpret the mental states of others, to empathise with their feelings, and to adopt their differing social perspectives. While there may be a degree of imprecision in the definition of these skills, it is clear that they are all important for the development of prosocial behaviour. It is also safe to conclude that there are developmental stages in the acquisition of these skills, and individual differences in their development. An individual child's manifestation of an ability will depend not only on the stage of her development, but also, for example, on her socialisation experience and on the complexity or familiarity of the particular situation in which the skill is required.

Communication skills

Fundamental to human social behaviour is the ability to communicate using language, a rule-governed symbol system, which allows us to share meanings with each other. Our social interactions and interpersonal relations are highly dependent upon our verbal ability to convey our knowledge, attitudes, preferences and feelings to each other. As reasonably successful adult communicators, we may take this skill for granted, but there are many difficulties facing the child learning to communicate with language. Of course, children must acquire the rules of the system, including an adequate vocabulary, a knowledge of the rules of grammar, and the physical capacity to produce speech sounds intelligibly. More important, however, is the acquisition of the conversational rules which govern the meaningful use of the language system. We use language to interact in so many ways – asking questions, making requests, issuing threats or promises, telling stories or jokes, giving instructions, and so on, and there are rules which determine the appropriate performance of each of these so-called 'speech acts', all of which require the active involvement of both speaker and listener to achieve mutual understanding. Consider just two aspects of successful communication, both of which pose problems for adults, let alone for children.

A speaker's task is to convey a message as unambiguously as possible to a listener. In order to do so, the speaker must assess not only how much the listener needs to know in order to understand, but also how best to convey this information in context. Suppose a teacher were to direct a pupil to collect something from her car outside the school by saying 'it's in the Rover'. This message would be effective if the pupil knows what a Rover looks like, and if the other cars in the playground were a Vauxhall, a Toyota and a Mini, but it would be ineffective if there were two Rovers parked outside.

From the listener's point of view, the task is to work out what a speaker means, often by drawing inferences. Speakers are necessarily selective in the information they convey, and listeners are left to fill in the gaps with what have been called 'bridging inferences'. For example, if I tell you that I went to a party last night and the room was smoky, you easily infer that the smoky room was where the party was held. However, if I were to say that I went to a party last night and that the dead man looked peaceful, you must build a bigger 'bridge' to infer that the party must have been a wake. Making bridging inferences clearly requires knowledge of the world and its possible connections, which children will lack. But they also lack inferencing skill itself, having difficulty in interpreting meaning beyond that which is explicitly presented.

In the context of children's peer groups, of course, many conversations are polyadic, not dyadic. The ability to participate in such group conversations requires that skills such as being able to *initiate* a conversation (with questions, suggestions or requests), to *maintain* a conversation (by making relevant contributions to the same topic), to *advance* a conversation (by requesting clarification, or giving constructive criticisms, elaborations or explanations) and to *complete* a conversation (by summarising and drawing conclusions) must be applied in the context of conventions governing turn-taking. Group conversational skill also demands different modes of talk, including the experiential ('I remember . . .'), the hypothetical ('suppose we did . . .'), the argumentative ('yes, but . . .') and the instructional or explanatory ('this is how . . .'); and perhaps most important, it requires socially supportive contributions fostering group cohesion, by offering positive feedback and encouragement ('that's a good idea'; 'what do you think?').

Successful communication therefore requires that speakers and listeners are in reciprocal negotiation with each other, respectively seeking and giving feedback about the meanings being conveyed, clarifying ambiguities and checking interpretations. Interpersonal communication is a skill in which children need a great deal of practice, and in which there is most potential for learning. One of the benefits of the peer interaction discussion tasks which we shall describe later in this book, is that they will encourage children to develop these skills, and to recognise and consider perspectives different from their own.

While mind-reading, empathising, role-taking and communicating all form part of successful social interaction, the making of friendships involves something more, namely, a psychological attachment, the development of feelings of trust, and an understanding of the rules, obligations and benefits of such particular relationships. The formation of friendships contributes to a child's self-concept, confidence and self-esteem. Friendships afford children opportunities for social comparison, which is a means of discovery

Children's friendships

and of self-validation. Children's early social comparisons tend to focus on the physical domain – objects, traits or behaviours, and seem designed to establish solidarity with their peers by comparing their similarities (the 'me too' approach); they then begin to demonstrate an interest in contrasts or differences ('I'm not the same as you'; 'I'm doing it my way'). Somewhat later, comparisons become more psychological, exploring each others' feelings and preferences ('who do you like best?'). Such mutual self disclosure within friendship relations is an important aspect of socialisation, helping the child to gain a wider perspective on reality, and reducing the egocentricity of her own perception and understanding.

Given the importance of developing friendships, children who have good friendship-making skills will have an advantage, and the skills involved are very much those we have been considering – communication ability, role-taking skills, empathy, etc. It is therefore unsurprising that children who are popular have been found to be more skilled on referential communication tasks, to have higher levels of interpersonal understanding and affective role-taking – for example, they are more sensitive to the needs of others, and generally exhibit more prosocial behaviour.

A number of theorists have tried to characterise different stages in the nature of children's friendships (Damon 1977; Selman 1980). For example, in the early primary school years (5–8 years), children describe friends merely as those 'who live near you', 'who you play with', 'who help you'; and a primary motivating factor in choosing a friend seems to be the social status or popularity such friends bring. Later primary school friendships (9–11 years) are characterised more by shared interests and values, an awareness of differing emotions and intentions, and of reciprocity within the relationship, in terms of sharing, helping and affection; children's descriptions of friendship at this stage mention being accepted by their friends, and admiring a friend's qualities. Adolescent friendships bring increasing intimacy and self-disclosure, together with an awareness of interdependence and mutual autonomy, and of the loyalty and commitment that the relationship requires. While such developmental changes in children's conceptions of friendships undoubtedly occur, Judy Dunn (1993) has argued that we have tended to underestimate young children's social understanding, and she has provided good evidence that pre-school children can engage in insightful discussions of their social relationships.

Children who fail to form friendships, and who are neglected or even rejected by their peers are more likely to exhibit behavioural difficulties. While popular children develop the skills of cooperative play and social conversation, neglected or ignored children remain isolated from the group, and consequently lack practice in social interaction, and children who are actively rejected by their peers are more likely to be involved non-cooperatively or aggressively in social situations. The links between peer rejection and antisocial behaviour (and also academic failure) have been reasonably well established, although we must be wary of assuming either the inevitability of the link or its causal direction. For example, the antisocial behaviour loosely described as bullying can be a socially skilful means of acquiring group status, and there is growing evidence that antisocial children develop friendships with other antisocial children. However, children who exhibit unprovoked aggression, or children who are aggressive and who also lack social skills, do tend to be unpopular with their peers.

Prosocial behaviours are types of interaction which favour and foster social relationships. A consensual definition would include those behaviours which show respect, interest and concern for others, and which may be exemplified in helping, caring and sharing. It is a matter of importance to consider whether and how these behaviours can be encouraged in young children. The teaching strategies most frequently studied are *modelling*, *exhortation* and *reinforcement*, that is, the extent to which children's behaviour is influenced (a) by the behaviour of others, (b) by what they are told, and (c) by the consequences for themselves. Ideally, this question should be addressed by long-term longitudinal studies, which can better disentangle cause–effect relationships, but such studies are expensive and, consequently, rare. For example, studies have shown that mothers do provide positive reinforcement (praise, thanks or physical affection) for children's (aged 4–7 years) helping behaviour, and that there are individual differences between mothers in such provision, but it is less clear whether such reinforcement, or its absence, has an effect on children's later prosocial interactions. Other evidence confirms the common sense intuition that children will model their behaviour on that of the people who matter to them, on behaviours they observe firstly in their parents and later in their friends. However, the most interesting line of research, at least for the purposes of this book, is the potential relationship between children's prosocial behaviour and their reasoning and judgement about socio-moral rules, their understanding of right and wrong.

There are many rules of behaviour that children must learn in order to participate in social situations. These rules include the *social conventions* which facilitate interactions, such as appropriate gender roles and rules of politeness; *prudential rules*, such as those pertaining to road crossing behaviour and other safety situations, and *moral rules*, which are often held to be obligatory and universal, and which, by encouraging such behaviours as cooperation, mutual respect and altruism, and by placing constraints upon selfishness, aggression, etc., have consequences for the welfare of others. Children learn about conventional and moral rules from their own interactions, observations and play; in particular, they learn about rules from their violation in conflict situations with parents and peers. Conflicts with peers and siblings tend to be predominantly about moral issues – justice and fairness, aggression and kindness, whereas conflicts with

The development of moral understanding and prosocial behaviour

parents are more likely to be over manners and conventions of behaviour. Even pre-school children can make clear distinctions between moral and conventional rules. For example, when asked to make judgements about the hypothetical behaviours of individuals in stories, they can explain their judgements about moral rule violations in terms of fairness to others, saving others from harm, and appeasing one's conscience, whereas violations of social conventions are explained with reference to rules and authority (doing what you are told), to social cooperation (people should be nice), and to the need to avoid punishment. Significantly, when parents are inculcating rules in their children, they are more likely to present moral rules with explanations and justifications, whereas social rules are often given by diktat, without explanation.

How well do children understand the moral rules upon which social interaction depends? Most research on children's moral reasoning derives from the work of Piaget (1932) and Kohlberg (1976). Piaget presented children with a series of stories in which, for example, two child characters committed similar misdemeanours for different reasons, and he asked the children to make comparative judgements about the seriousness of these behaviours, and how they should be punished. On the basis of their replies, he produced a three-stage model of the development of moral thinking: (a) at the *pre-school stage*, children exhibit pre-moral judgement, in which they do not seem to understand the nature of rules; (b) in the stage of *moral realism* (5–9 years), rules are seen as fixed and immutable, and rule violations are judged in terms of consequences rather than intentions; (c) during the later stage of *moral subjectivism* (9 years upwards), children begin to judge the morality of an action in terms of its intentions more than its consequences, and realise that rules are socially created.

Kohlberg's approach was to present both child and adult subjects with hypothetical moral dilemmas, and ask them to explain and justify how they would resolve the dilemmas. His resulting model proposed three broad levels of moral understanding, each comprising two sub-stages. At the *pre-conventional level*, subjects reason from a perspective of self-interest, lacking an appreciation of society's expectations and conventions, and being principally concerned with avoiding punishment. This level corresponds to Piaget's moral realism, and mainly applies to children under 9 years, although some adolescents and antisocial adults may remain at this level. The level of *conventional morality* applies to most adolescents and adults in our society; here such considerations as trust and loyalty, having good motives, concern for others' welfare, the reciprocity of responsibilities, and acting in accordance with the dictates of conscience all begin to appear. At the *post-conventional level*, Kohlberg suggests that moral reasoning invokes underlying ethical principles rather than conventions, and takes account of the relativity of values and opinions.

Although both these models have been influential, they have received a number of criticisms. Children's moral reasoning does show a stage-like development, much as the theories describe, but children's thinking will always be underestimated by tasks which lack relevance to them, whereas, when a moral judgement has personal significance, children tend to reason at a higher level. Kohlberg's dilemmas typically focused upon an hypothetical conflict between different, obligatory responsibilities of the story characters, for example, should a child steal a medicine for his sick parent? An objection to such dilemmas is that they posit two undesirable alternatives – to steal, or to show a lack of care. More familiar dilemmas, however, usually involve conflict between responsibility (what we ought to do) and desire (what we want to do). Practical moral decision making takes place in the context of interpersonal relations and friendship, and recent research has therefore focused upon interpersonal moral reasoning, the development of children's moral orientation, and their ability to see the moral implications of interpersonal conflicts. We must also acknowledge cultural differences in the relationship between morality and behaviour, in terms of the importance attached to individual autonomy, material self-interest, tradition, community and religious norms, and so forth. Gilligan (1982) has further suggested a gender difference between Kohlberg's 'morality of justice, or ethical principles', which is male-orientated, and a 'morality of care', which favours the female perspective.

In conclusion, the two issues which motivate this book are the development of children's socio-moral awareness, and the relationship between such awareness and prosocial behaviour. Can we improve children's interpersonal sensitivity and understanding, and what effect would such improvement have upon their prosocial behaviour? There are grounds for optimism on both counts. Research has demonstrated the positive value of peer interaction on children's learning in a variety of educational domains, from understanding in primary science and mathematics to the acquisition of socio-moral and legal concepts. Of particular relevance here are studies which have shown that the discussion of moral dilemmas can produce improvements in moral reasoning scores (Damon and Killen 1982; Kruger and Tomasello 1986). Furthermore, children at higher levels of moral reasoning also tend to exhibit more prosocial behaviour (Eisenberg-Berg and Hand 1979). Our rationale for what follows, therefore, is that, by regularly providing children with an opportunity, in structured tasks, to discuss amongst themselves the motives, consequences and morality of interpersonal conflicts, we can thereby facilitate their socio-moral reasoning, which will in turn enhance their prosocial behaviours.

Chapter 2

Education for Personal and Social Development in Context

The social context

Within the context of growing concerns about standards of behaviour and morality amongst children, teachers, together with others in the caring professions, are increasingly being called upon to help individual children and families with serious social and emotional problems. Schools regularly find themselves having to deal with challenging antisocial behaviour among children and adolescents (teachers themselves having been victims of violent attacks in some cases); they are asked to help tackle crime and drug abuse in communities; and they are called upon to be in the front line both to detect and cope with child abuse in its various forms. In essence, what is now being expected of teachers and schools by society is that they should play a more vigorous role in averting what is seen as a general collapse in moral values and standards of behaviour.

Generally speaking, it would appear that the social world is perceived as an increasingly dangerous place. Much has been written about how the fears of parents for their children's safety are being translated into curbs on children's freedom. Children's leisure activity is constrained by what some see as almost a siege mentality among parents. For increasing numbers of children spare time is spent in relative social isolation in the home watching TV and playing video games. Hence, opportunities for the acquisition of social skills in interaction with the peer group are lost. There are also concerns about the quality of social experience provided for children within the family. Relationships are coming under pressure from many quarters, producing for large numbers of children the kinds of instability and insecurity often seen as being associated with the development of inappropriate patterns of social behaviour. Thus teachers may feel that they not only have to cope with the effects of inadequate socialisation but also that they are expected in some way to compensate for, and even remediate, their pupils' lack of relevant social experience in the curricular activities they provide.

These developments in the social context of childhood experience present a major potential challenge to the school curriculum. Schools, under pressure to deliver results in what are seen as the core academic subjects of the curriculum, may find it hard to rise to the challenge of attaching greater priority to personal and social education. Indeed, presented with what are perceived as extreme forms of unacceptable behaviour, it would appear that more and more schools are in this regard opting out, in that they find themselves resorting to the strategy of exclusion from school for an increasing number of 'difficult' children. However, as will be discussed in the following section, schools' obligations in the area of personal and social development are now inescapable.

The curriculum context

It is customary to differentiate between the formal, explicit, overt curriculum on the one hand and the informal, implicit or hidden curriculum on the other. Issues to do with children's social behaviour can be addressed at both the formal and the informal level. At the formal level, personal and social education (PSE) may be designated as an area of 'pastoral' curriculum or as a 'subject' in its own right, for example, being given a 'slot' in the timetables of secondary schools. However, it is often the case, especially in primary schools, that personal and social development (PSD) is seen as more informal, permeating the rest of the curriculum (Tattum and Tattum 1992). Both of these alternatives need to be explored in order to clarify the context for suggested strategies for teaching social behaviour.

Since the late 1980s, there has been an unprecedented amount of Government effort devoted to the formalising of curricular advice to schools in the UK, culminating in England and Wales in a National Curriculum for all school children up to school leaving age and in Scotland, in National Guidelines applying to the education of all children aged 5 to 14. What is the place of PSE within these formal curricular frameworks? In the case of Scotland, schools now have a set of National Guidelines for Personal and Social Development (SOED 1993). According to these guidelines, personal and social development can be divided into *personal development*, comprising knowledge, skills and attitudes associated with *self-awareness* and *self-esteem* and *social development*, comprising knowledge, skills and attitudes associated with *interpersonal relationships* and *independence/interdependence*. Each of these four areas is elaborated by providing examples of pupils' potential development. For example, in terms of interpersonal relationships, Table 2.1 indicates the kinds of statements provided in the guidelines against which the curriculum for PSD can be developed and pupils' progress judged. Each row represents a separate strand of development, and progression is shown in adjacent statements reading from left to right. What marks progression in the complete set of statements seems to be an increasing expectation that children will engage in reflection and evaluation of their own social behaviour, their experiences of interpersonal relationships, and their developing system of values.

Table 2.1 Examples of pupils' potential development: interpersonal relationships

Be aware that each person has a number of roles →	Adopt different roles within groups →	Reflect on and evaluate their own roles and those of others
Demonstrate an awareness of family relationships →	Demonstrate an awareness that specific factors such as gender can affect inter-personal relationships →	Identify the different kinds of relationships that exist between the sexes
Communicate and interact with known persons →	Communicate and interact with growing confidence within a wider circle of people →	Communicate and interact by selecting and using effectively a range of interpersonal skills in a variety of situations
Begin to identify values which are important to the home, school and community →	Express their own views on values which are important to the home, school and community →	Reflect upon, evaluate and express their opinion about values held by the school and the community
Demonstrate respect and tolerance towards others →	Demonstrate respect and tolerance for those whose opinions differ from their own →	Evaluate and demonstrate the acquisition of positive attitudes to others

(SOED 1993, p. 12)

On the surface some of these statements appear unremarkable. However, closer examination of the practical implications of adopting them as targets for curriculum planning suggests that they carry considerable challenges. The bald statement, 'demonstrate respect and tolerance towards others', is a good example of something which is really a fundamental educational aim, but which might all too readily be simply taken for granted and sadly overlooked. Just as in any other area of the curriculum, if such 'targets' are to be taken seriously, effort will have to be devoted to planning, implementing and evaluating appropriate learning experiences. If we are committed to progression in PSD we must plan progressively challenging programmes of study in this domain and not simply assume that somehow it will all just come about spontaneously. The 5–14 guidelines suggest that much can be achieved informally through the creation of a positive class and school ethos. However, they also point to the need to provide specific learning opportunities designed to enable children to acquire and practise social skills by, for example, expressing their personal perspective on relationships and considering the appropriate form of interaction in different social contexts (SOED 1993, p. 13).

Two years after the appearance of the National Guidelines for PSD 5–14 the Scottish Consultative Council on the Curriculum (SCCC) contributed significantly to the debate by producing their paper entitled, *The Heart of the Matter: Education for Personal and Social Development: A Paper for Discussion and Development* (SCCC 1995). The paper argues that education for PSD should be a central concern for all those involved in schooling and that this should be promoted through a synthesis of three elements which echo the advice of the 5–14 guidelines, namely:

- fostering a positive whole-school climate and ethos;
- adopting the kinds of approaches to teaching and learning which will enhance PSD;
- finding appropriate locations in the curriculum to deal with issues in, and aspects of, PSD.

The SCCC (1995) paper asserts that, as far as education for PSD is concerned, there is a core set of key qualities or dispositions, which it elsewhere describes as principles for values in education (SCCC 1991). These are:

- respect and caring for self;
- respect and caring for others;
- a sense of social responsibility;
- a commitment to learning; and
- a sense of belonging.

The paper also identifies vital skills, knowledge and understanding essential for the personal growth involved in PSD as implied by the key qualities. Significant among these are personal, interpersonal and communication skills, and knowledge and understanding from the perspectives of 'self', 'relationships', 'rights and responsibilities' and 'work' (SCCC 1995, pp. 6–7). In education for PSD, learning and teaching should, in other words, focus on the knowledge and understandings children need to be able to function effectively as individuals in 'considerate and supportive relationships' to cope with the demands of adult life and to contribute to society.

In England and Wales the National Curriculum Council acknowledges in its guidance to schools the importance of PSD as a dimension of the school curriculum (NCC 1990a). More specifically in its guidance on Education for Citizenship (Curriculum Guidance 8), there is recognition of the importance of fostering 'personal and social skills' together with the promotion of 'positive attitudes, moral codes and values' (NCC 1990b, p. 4), the latter aspects of the available curricular advice being taken further in *Spiritual and Moral Education: A Discussion Paper* (NCC 1993). Though still relatively scarce, resources are now becoming available to support this area of the school curriculum. For example, as a result of collaboration between the Citizenship Foundation and the Home Office, a comprehensive resource pack for social and moral responsibility, *You, Me, Us!*, has been issued to primary schools (Rowe and Newton 1994). In their approach to citizenship education, Rowe and Newton recognise the close relationship between social and moral development. In their view children's moral development can be measured in terms of the degree to which they can show:

an understanding of the difference between right and wrong; respect for persons, truth and property; a concern for how their actions may affect others; the ability to make responsible and reasoned judgements on moral issues; and moral behaviour. (p. 5)

Children's social development, on the other hand, will be reflected in:

> the quality of relationships in the school; pupils' ability to exercise a degree of responsibility and initiative; pupils' ability to work successfully in groups and to participate cooperatively and productively in the school community; and pupils' growing understanding of society through the family, the school and the local and wider communities, leading to an understanding of the structures and processes of society. (Rowe and Newton 1994, p. 5)

According to Rowe and Newton, teachers find moral education particularly challenging and, therefore, resort to what is referred to as 'the school ethos approach', in other words a more implicit approach which would include ideas such as: 'establishing a caring school; setting out clear and reasonable rules of conduct which the children can recognise as fair; setting examples of good, caring behaviour; and using RE and assemblies to provide some moral teaching' (page b).

However, it is argued that, while these are essential steps, much more needs to be done to provide children with genuine opportunities to explore social and moral issues and to enter into the kind of dialogue with others which will reveal both differences and similarities in moral perspectives and which in turn will foster the tolerance and respect for diversity which is essential in our pluralist society (Rowe and Newton 1994).

In discussing how its aims for this area of the curriculum can be achieved, SCCC (1995) acknowledges that education for PSD presents major challenges for curriculum development, institutional development and personal professional development. It encourages discussion of priorities and strategies among all parties, including parents. In the spirit of opening such a dialogue, the ideas contained in the rest of the chapters of this book are offered not as solutions to the problem of teaching social behaviour, but as suggestions for discussion and experimentation.

Alternative educational strategies for teaching positive social behaviour

In the current context of concern about children's social behaviour there is, therefore, a need to identify ways to provide educational experiences which will foster interpersonal skills. There has perhaps been a tendency to assume that these skills will simply develop spontaneously and that there is little scope for educational intervention in this domain. There are cultural explanations for a lack of concern for matters to do with interpersonal relationships in general and prosocial behaviour in particular. Gardner (1983) in his theory of 'multiple intelligences' identifies significant cultural differences with respect to the 'personal intelligences' in which are included both interpersonal (involving social awareness, ability to empathise and interact effectively) and intrapersonal (involving self-awareness and emotional sensitivity) forms. According to Gardner, in Western societies the personal intelligences are de-emphasised in comparison with logico-mathematical and other forms of intelligence, and within the personal domain the interpersonal receives less stress than the intrapersonal in our predominantly 'atomised' society (Gardner 1983). The appearance of PSD/PSE in curricular advice signals an opportunity to plan for educational provision in this neglected field. Indeed the SCCC in its choice of title for its discussion paper on education for PSD has signified the central role of this aspect of the curriculum by calling it 'The Heart of the Matter' (SCCC 1995).

What then can schools do to provide appropriate learning experiences for children in the domain of interpersonal relationships? General exhortations to schools to strive for a more positive ethos provide an important and worthwhile aspiration, but they are not sufficiently specific in themselves. Teachers require practical solutions to the challenge of delivering an effective curriculum for this aspect of the PSE of the children in their care. Advice which calls for PSD to become a dimension of all curricular activities might seem persuasive, but similarly lacks specificity. More specific methods which educators might adopt to promote positive relationships and interpersonal behaviour within the curriculum might include:

- developing strategies for the management of social behaviour in the classroom;
- providing practical learning activities aimed at improving interpersonal skills;
- providing learning activities specifically designed to encourage children to think about, and thereby enhance, their understanding of interpersonal relationships;
- finding opportunities to encourage children to discuss moral values in the domain of relationships; and
- providing an appropriate 'real' context in which children can display genuinely prosocial behaviour.

Of course, these strategies are not mutually exclusive. Indeed it could be argued that ideally they should all be considered and, where possible, integrated into a coherent curricular approach which will help to create a positive, caring classroom climate. However, for the sake of clarity, the different strategies will be dealt with in turn. We shall look briefly at some of the available advice relevant to each strategy, and at the kinds of factors which might influence its effective implementation.

Management of social behaviour in the classroom

While the family is generally seen as the main socialising influence on children, the school also provides a vitally important social arena in which socialisation takes place. Tattum and Tattum (1992) describe the influences provided by the school as the 'social curriculum' through which children can learn a great deal about interpersonal relationships as well as standards for their social behaviour. Adult members of the school community are potentially powerful models of social behaviour, both of the desirable and the undesirable variety.

Consistency, fairness, respect and caring for others are attributes which can be consciously cultivated and demonstrated in a teacher's day-to-day interactions with children, and children themselves can be encouraged to display such qualities in their own social interactions.

In the 'behavioural' approach to classroom discipline (Wheldall and Merrett 1984), the emphasis is on finding ways to positively reinforce desired behaviours. The approach entails a number of key variables which are susceptible to manipulation by the teacher. Principally there are three main elements from which the acronym, 'the ABC approach', is derived, namely, Antecedents, Behaviour and Consequences. The antecedents are the context, the conditions, in which the behaviour takes place. Behaviour can clearly be influenced by manipulating the antecedent conditions. A much mentioned example of this is changing the classroom seating arrangement from tables to rows. In situations where the teacher wishes children to engage in an individual learning activity, it has been found that seating in rows can lead to increased 'on-task' behaviour compared with seating in social groups. This is not to say that the behavioural approach necessarily advocates one particular form of seating arrangement. Rather it argues for the antecedent conditions to be set appropriately for the desired behaviour, whatever that might be. Clearly if the desired behaviour were some form of collaborative activity, the ideal seating arrangement might be quite different from that demanded were individual activity required. Another way in which the context can be manipulated in order to foster desired behaviours is by providing a clear set of rules for classroom behaviour, the effectiveness of which may be influenced by the extent to which the children themselves have been involved in their construction.

The hallmark of the behavioural approach is its emphasis on the manipulation of the consequences of behaviour by way of positive reinforcement and its assumption that an individual will be likely to repeat a behaviour if that behaviour produces favourable consequences. This idea is uncontroversial and indeed may seem too obvious to mention in relation to the complex social context of the school classroom. Teachers might tend to assume that they use positive reinforcement without having to think about it. However, Wheldall and his colleagues conducted a series of naturalistic observational studies in classrooms which showed that the spontaneous amount of teacher praise (one possible form of positive reinforcement) was in fact very low in many classrooms, even where the teachers claimed that they praised as a matter of course. Specifically what was found was that teachers did tend to give praise for good 'academic' behaviour (i.e. for work well done: a good drawing, or a page of accurate calculations), but did not as often praise children for their good social behaviour which, it seemed, was simply taken for granted – a finding replicated in research by the present authors which will be reported in Chapter 3. On the other hand, they were highly likely to punish, by means of verbal reprimand, any bad social behaviour exhibited by children in class. The prevailing view among those who subscribe to the behavioural approach is that the use of punishment, as well as being ethically questionable, is less effective in shaping and maintaining desirable behaviours than the consistent and appropriate use of positive reinforcement. The logic of this view underlines the importance, in the domain of social behaviour, of finding ways to reinforce prosocial behaviour, rather than merely punishing antisocial behaviour.

Fostering moral values in the classroom

A great deal of interest has been shown in recent years in 'values education'. There have been recent public demands for action by schools to counter what is seen as a collapse of moral values. Politicians have sought the cooperation of teachers in their attempt to get rid of the scourge of moral relativism, to identify a core of fundamental values on which all 'decent' individuals might agree, and to introduce these into the curriculum in order to provide children with a proper framework for knowing what is right and what is wrong. Of course, this enterprise is fraught with difficulty. Indeed as Mary Warnock points out in her book, *The Uses of Philosophy* (Warnock 1992), the quest for a moral consensus has exercised philosophers for centuries without any clear conclusions. She concludes that in the absence of a general moral consensus in society, the best we can do about moral differences is to try to keep talking, not in the hope that the differences will somehow be ironed out, but in the hope that the differences can be accommodated within a broadly law-abiding society. Nevertheless the idea of seeking a core set of shared or 'fundamental' values seems to remain a powerful force among current educational policy makers and shapers.

A major study, commissioned by the Gordon Cook Foundation, was carried out by the Scottish Council for Research in Education on values education in the primary school (Powney *et al.* 1995). From a series of in-depth case studies of selected primary schools and a wider questionnaire survey, the authors concluded that there was indeed evidence of common, shared values being promoted by staff in their pupils, such values being expressed in 'broad, overlapping terms, such as caring, consideration and respect for others, self-esteem, cooperation, good manners and work' (p. *viii*) These terms largely appear to denote desirable personal attributes or social behaviours and it was in terms of pupil behaviour that teachers measured the success of the values education they were providing.

In their appraisal of the way values were conceptualised and fostered by teachers, Powney *et al.* had looked for three different aspects, namely, behaviour, feelings and cognition, but failed to find much evidence of the cognitive aspect being engaged and at best found only implicit treatment of the emotional aspect. Pupils tended not to be explicitly encouraged to think about their own knowledge and understanding in the moral domain or to consider the process of arriving at a 'personal stance' on moral issues. The conclusion to be drawn from this important primary school study is that there is considerable scope for a more explicit treatment of all aspects of values in classrooms. Social behaviour may be a 'natural' starting point, providing a suitable focus for discussion. Children should be given opportunities to analyse their social experiences in more depth, actively and constructively reflecting on such matters and articulating reasons for moral decisions. Chapters 5 to 8 of this book are intended to provide stimulus material and suggested strategies to foster such activity.

Enhancing children's understanding of interpersonal relationships

Given the key significance of peer relationships in the process of socialisation, and the well-documented advantages to be gained from peer learning, it would seem desirable to devise activities which enable children to explore their own understandings of relationships by sharing them constructively with peers. Chapters 6 and 7 will present a range of activities of this kind which can be adapted for use in most educational contexts. Dunn (1993) argues that we have tended to underestimate young children's social understanding and provides compelling evidence of the ability of pre-school children to engage in insightful discussion of their social relationships. However, school children, perhaps through lack of opportunity, give the appearance of being ill-equipped to talk about their experiences of interpersonal relationships. As a first step, ways should be found to foster such conversations in order to challenge children to think about their own and others' attitudes, motives, intentions and behaviour. Adalbjarnardottir (1994) encouraged teachers to provide children with a problem-solving structure for the resolution of interpersonal difficulties and the discussion of socio-moral issues in the classroom. The emphasis in this apparently effective programme was on discussion of different perspectives on social relationships, and the stimulus materials in this book are designed to be a focus for similar activities.

School bullying – a catalyst for school development

Alongside the concerns about children behaving antisocially, which we discussed at the beginning of this chapter, there has been a parallel development of concern on behalf of children as *victims* of antisocial behaviour. Child protection has become a major focus for government legislation (Children Act, 1989 and Children (Scotland) Act, 1995) and policy making in the caring professions. Schools have a duty of care towards children to ensure that they have a safe, secure environment for learning. A particular focus of concern over the past few years has been the issue of school bullying, an area which was relatively neglected in the UK by both researchers and practitioners until the late 1980s. Following the pioneering efforts of Dan Olweus in Scandinavia, the work of Peter Smith and his colleagues, carried out at the University of Sheffield, has lead the way in this country (Olweus 1993; Smith and Thompson 1991; Smith and Sharp 1994).

Many resource packages designed to facilitate anti-bullying strategies have been developed. The first of these to be issued to all schools was produced by the Scottish Council for Research in Education (Johnstone *et al.* 1991). This has been followed by many more, some sponsored by central or local government agencies (e.g. Department for Education 1994; McLean 1991, 1994); some produced by commercial publishers (e.g. Brock 1992); and some by charitable bodies (e.g. Kidscape 1994; Childline 1994). The consensus among these sources of advice is that schools should develop a whole-school policy involving all parties in raising awareness of the nature and prevalence of bullying and in tackling the problem accordingly. In a fully effective anti-bullying policy, however, not only must appropriate steps be taken to combat bullying by equipping all parties to deal effectively with any bullying incidents which may arise, but there must also be a clear attempt to create conditions in the school which will foster positive interpersonal relationships in such a way as to make bullying less likely to occur. In other words, prevention of bullying in schools will require attention to be paid to encouraging prosocial behaviours as well as inhibiting the antisocial behaviour. The need for a broader preventative approach is highlighted by a recent longitudinal study which monitored the levels of reported bullying in schools which had been involved in anti-bullying intervention programmes (Thompson 1995). This study illustrated the relative intractability of the problem in that most of the schools involved found it difficult to sustain the initial reductions in the rate of incidence of bullying over a period of two years following the introduction of the anti-bullying policy.

However, there should be a direct link between a preventative anti-bullying policy, on the one hand, and school policy concerned with PSD and PSE on the other. Indeed it can be argued that the issue of bullying, as it affects such a large number of children either directly or indirectly, is an appropriate starting point for discussion of socio-moral questions and a suitable point of entry for consideration of interpersonal relationships and conflict. While a great deal of resource material directed at the problem of bullying is now available to schools, there is a need for well focused activities which will enable children to go beyond simply dealing with this particular problem in social behaviour to gain a broader understanding of the whole spectrum of interpersonal relationships.

It is important to stress that if education for PSD is really to be seen as 'the heart of the matter' of the school curriculum, then its importance must apply equally to all children. In some ways the potential problems of antisocial behaviour are particularly severe for those who have special educational needs. There is evidence, for example, that there is a greater probability that children with special educational needs will find themselves the victims of bullying (Whitney *et al.* 1992; Thompson *et al.* 1994). The research suggests two

Socio-moral education is for all children

relevant factors; firstly, that the particular character of these children's needs may be used as an excuse for bullying, and secondly, that children with special needs typically have fewer friends and are less well integrated socially in the group. Other institutional factors may also influence the quality of social interaction experienced by children who have special educational needs. The trend towards integration into mainstream educational contexts may have different implications for individual children according to how well the process of integration is managed. Of course, many children will continue to receive at least part of their education in special school settings and while teachers in the special school sector have tended to place heavier emphasis on PSD than their counterparts in mainstream schools, there is still a need for good resources which can support consideration of interpersonal relationships in these settings.

Finding a practical context for teaching positive social behaviour: a community focus?

The SCCC (1995) discussion paper suggests that education for PSD should be central to all teaching and learning, and stresses the importance of creating an ethos of 'inclusiveness' (p. 10) in order to make a school effective in this regard. An inclusive school is one in which all feel they are respected and valued, a school which takes account of 'the perspectives of parents, of the wider community and of the young people themselves' (p. 10), in other words, a caring community. It is affirmed in the paper that children who feel this sense of belonging to their school, of being cared for, and included, are more likely to be responsible individuals with an appreciation of the value of service to the community and helping others. These are fine words. Again one might ask how the rhetoric can be followed through into actual learning in the domain of social development. As noted above, the notion of 'citizenship education' has found itself back in the vocabulary of the curriculum. Perhaps having opportunities to learn how to be a 'good citizen' might enable children to acquire socially responsible behaviours and moral values. This and other ideas about practical contexts for teaching social behaviour will be explored in Chapter 8.

The concept of community service has very negative connotations in our culture. The unfortunate association seems to be with crime and punishment, with community service being seen as an alternative to a prison sentence rather than something of intrinsic value in its own right. In many other countries working for the community is a significant element in the life experience of children and adolescents. During a recent food poisoning epidemic in Japan, for example, attention was drawn to the practice of children taking responsibility for the preparation and serving of food for their peers in schools. The value attached to such service in Japanese culture is very high.

Shared responsibilities in the community remain an accepted part of daily life in the Israeli kibbutz. For example, in Kibbutz Yagur from the age of twelve, children work two afternoons a week for the community without pay; secondary school children fulfil their responsibilities by working one full day per week in the community; from the age of fourteen children take responsibility as youth leaders for the younger children, being responsible for all their leisure time activities after school and during school holidays; for older children this service to the community extends to working for half of every vacation wherever they may be needed on the kibbutz (K. Smith 1996, personal communication).

While many children have work responsibilities (and child labour abuses are well documented), and many carry significant responsibilities within the family for the care of younger siblings or even parents who suffer from illness or disability, such structured involvement in community work as in the case of the kibbutz would be seen as highly unusual in the UK. Nevertheless, the concept of service in the community may provide a channel for curricular planning which genuinely addresses the kinds of aspirations implicit in official guidelines and stated school policies for personal and social development.

Chapter 3

Children's Prosocial Behaviour

If our intention is to foster children's prosocial behaviour and to inhibit their antisocial behaviour, then we must begin by giving some consideration to the behaviours to which these labels are deemed to apply, and the extent to which there is consensus about their definition and use. Although these categories may initially seem to be clear and self-evident, a moment's reflection should remind us that we very often differ in our attitudes towards certain child social behaviours. And if parents or teachers can differ in what they think of as good or bad child behaviour, then it seems most probable that adults and children will also differ in their views. Of course, there will be clear-cut examples about which we would all agree. However, the interpretation of social behaviours is determined so much by the attitudes and values, not only of the broader cultural community, but also of a variety of sub-cultures – the family, peer groups, etc. – that it soon becomes clear that there is ample scope for the development of different perceptions and interpretations of children's social behaviour. In this chapter we will examine what seems to be meant by children's prosocial behaviours, and in the following chapter we shall turn our attention to definitions of their antisocial behaviours.

Prosocial behaviours may be uncontroversially defined as those behaviours in which an individual uses his or her own resources to achieve positive outcomes for someone else. We might agree that *helping* is a good example of such behaviour. However, such apparent consensus becomes less certain when we remember that, although helping behaviour may attract support in principle, it can, in certain contexts, receive more negative interpretations such as conformity ('he's only trying to fit in, to be accepted') or attention-seeking ('she's only doing that because we are watching'). As with helping, so too our interpretations of other apparently prosocial behaviours can differ, and different interpretations, of course, lead to different responses. The feedback, approval or disapproval, that children receive in relation to their social behaviours will therefore depend upon the respondent's interpretation of that behaviour.

Suppose a teacher witnessed the following event in her classroom.

Johnny, aged eight, is having difficulty with his sums, and he solicits help from his neighbour, Billy. Billy refuses to help, but Annie, across the table, volunteers assistance, which Johnny vehemently rejects. The teacher's interpretation of Annie's behaviour is that she was being kind, supportive and helpful; she therefore commends Annie and reprimands Johnny for his ingratitude. However, Johnny hadn't see it like that; his pride was at stake and, from his viewpoint, Annie was being an interfering girl whose assistance wasn't wanted. Whereas Billy, who was apparently being unhelpful, had seen the teacher watching and was actually trying to protect Johnny from getting into trouble. And what about Annie? Was she upset by Johnny's rejection of her well-intended offer, or had she actually been taking the opportunity to show how smart she was, and to put Johnny down? Such interactions are, of course, commonplace among children, but they highlight two problems for any attempt to manage children's social behaviour. Most obviously, there is the question of how to interpret a child's actions: is this an action of which we broadly approve or disapprove, that we identify as prosocial or antisocial? And secondly, how, if at all, should we show our approval or disapproval of the behaviour? The above example also reminds us that interpreting a child's social behaviour involves an assessment of the actor's intentions as well as her actions, that different people can have different views about the same behaviour, and that responding appropriately to a child's behaviour with either approval or disapproval depends upon an accurate interpretation of its intent.

It was with these questions in mind that we conducted a survey of children (in the age range 9–13 years), their parents and their teachers, in both mainstream and special education, to discover their different experiences of children's prosocial and antisocial behaviours. We asked these different groups to describe, from their own experiences, what they considered to be examples of children behaving well or badly. In so doing, we hoped to discover which prosocial and antisocial child behaviours seemed most salient to them, and whether they differed in their views. Children were asked to describe incidents in which another child had (a) been nice to them, or done something that pleased them, and (b) been nasty to them, or done something to upset them. Teachers were asked to describe similar episodes which they had witnessed or had reported to them in their class. Parents described examples of child behaviours they had witnessed, or which their own child had reported having experienced or witnessed. At this point, readers may wish to pause and recall their own experiences of children behaving well. What examples come to mind, and why? How, if at all, did you react to the child whose behaviour impressed you?

A total of 200 examples of children behaving well were elicited from the various groups, and content analysed to identify recognisable categories of prosocial behaviours. Such a task has been attempted before. For example, Eisenberg-Berg and Hand (1979) recorded observations of pre-school children's prosocial behaviour under the headings *sharing*, *helping*, *offers comfort*, and *acts sociably*. Marantz (1988) in her review of intervention studies aiming to foster prosocial behaviour in young schoolchildren, cites *sharing, donating, cooperating, helping others in distress, comforting, sympathising* and *volunteering to help.* The categories which emerged from the content analysis of our examples were *sharing, helping, caring* and *inclusion.* As may be seen from their definition in Table 3.1, these categories are very similar to those of Eisenberg-Berg and Hand, and subsume most of those cited by Marantz.

Table 3.1 Categories of prosocial behaviour, and their definitions, from elicited descriptions

Category	Definition
Sharing	Sharing possessions, giving gifts
Helping	Physical or practical help, e.g. with schoolwork, or after an accident; Samaritan acts
Caring	Psychological support, sympathy or comfort; empathy; loyalty
Inclusion	Befriending, making someone welcome; playing with, talking to, preventing isolation

While we cannot be certain whether a particular behaviour was cited because it was a really striking example, or because it was a frequent experience, there were some notable differences between the groups in the kind of prosocial behaviours they described. These differences are briefly summarised in Table 3.2, and will be considered in more detail in the following sections. Briefly, Table 3.2 shows that teachers, particularly in special schools, mentioned *helping behaviours* much more often than did parents or children; that parents and teachers both gave far more examples of *caring behaviours* than did the children; that *sharing* seemed quite salient for children, less so for parents, and hardly at all for teachers, and that *inclusion* was the prosocial behaviour most commonly mentioned by children overall, and much more often by children in special schools than by those in mainstream schools.

Table 3.2 Percentage of examples of each prosocial category provided by each subject group

	Children		Parents		Teachers	
	Mainstream	Special	Mainstream	Special	Mainstream	Special
Sharing	22	16	14	13	7	4
Helping	27	11	29	17	41	57
Caring	18	7	32	39	35	35
Inclusion	33	66	25	30	17	4

By far the most commonly cited behaviours were examples of *inclusion*, in which children narrated their experiences of being befriended or included in other children's activities. In other words, as a consequence of this prosocial behaviour, its recipient had company and was not isolated. However, it is not only the consequence of the behaviour that matters, but also the actor's deliberate intention to offer company. This distinction between intention and outcome can be noted by contrasting the *inclusion* examples given by children in mainstream and special schools. The examples of special school children predominantly involved playing with someone, and focused largely on the consequences for the recipient (having a playmate), without identifying the intentional component: 'they just played with me' (13-year-old boy); 'playing with me at computer games' (14-year-old boy); 'they played ball with me' (9-year-old boy); 'they played with me – hide and seek' (14-year-old girl); 'they might play with me' (9-year-old boy). The element of keeping someone company was sometimes made more explicit, as in: 'talk to me and take me for a game of football' (14-year-old boy); 'go to the swing park, and play together' (9-year-old boy); 'Steven comes to my house to play with me' (9-year-old boy). However, the actor's volition was only rarely made apparent, in such examples as: 'they ask me to play with them' (12-year-old boy); 'she asked me to go to the baths' (14-year-old girl); 'they invited me to their party" (10-year-old girl). On a rather different note, the social interaction that apparently pleased one 14-year-old boy was 'we just go and annoy people'.

Readers may recall from Chapter 1 that it is a growing awareness of other people's intentions that characterises children's developing understanding of mind and, in this respect, the above examples contrast with the *inclusion* behaviours cited by children in mainstream education, which invariably made explicit the actor's intention (and were also, and understandably, not so narrowly focused upon 'playing together'): 'I was invited to a birthday party' (12-year-old girl); 'Gillian asks me if I want to go out with her at weekends' (12-year-old girl); 'my friend let me stay at her house and I had a good time' (13-year-old girl); 'when I first started this school, they made friends with me' (11-year-old girl); 'when they ask you to go places like swimming or the pictures' (11-year-old girl); 'they let me play football' (12-year-old boy); 'it was raining and my pal said – are you coming down to my house now?' (12-year-old boy). The other notable feature of the mainstream children's examples was their willingness to offer explanations as to why they liked these behaviours. These explanations ranged from the insightful 'she was being friendly and caring', 'that's nice, 'cause they want to be with you and that', 'because they were counting me in', to the revealing "cause they weren't fighting with us', and "cause we're doing as we're told'.

Helping behaviours were mentioned frequently by mainstream children, less often by children in special schools. Mainstream examples included help with schoolwork ('in class if you're doing work that's difficult, they'll explain it to you'), giving directions ('when I first come to this school, everyone showed me all the places'), help after an accident ('when I fell off my bike and cut my hand, my friend took my bike home for me'), and giving general assistance ('when I lost my jotter they helped me to look for it'). Again, the children's explanations ('why do you think this was "nice" behaviour?') were revealing 'they could have put my jotter in a puddle, but they gave it back', 'in other classes they let you do it yourself', 'other children would just have left me'. Special school children's *helping* examples included help with schoolwork, giving directions, and also physical assistance with a disability ('she lifted me on my chair').

Social interactions which involved *sharing*, giving or lending were quite popular with both groups of children. In the case of special school children, the examples were of only minor transactions such as sharing a playpiece or giving sweets, and lending was not mentioned. A single, interesting exception to these somewhat mundane examples was given by one 9-year-old boy – 'my pal gave me motors, but I had to pay for them' – who seemed well aware that such limited generosity was not a good example of 'nice' behaviour. Mainstream children talked about sharing (sweets and things), giving (presents, money when needed) and lending (money or games), and some were able to give perceptive explanations 'It's nice to think someone cares enough to give you presents', 'instead of putting it to waste, he lent it (a computer) to me while he was away'.

The final category, *caring*, might be considered to be the basis for all prosocial behaviour and friendly relations, insofar as attempts to share, to help or to include arise from a caring attitude. Although examples of caring behaviours were less often mentioned by the children, the mainstream children clearly showed an understanding of their importance within social relationships. Their examples focused primarily on behaviours directed at the recipient's emotional wellbeing: 'if anything bad happens, she talks it over with me' (12-year-old girl); 'when my dad died, everyone was nice to me' (13-year-old girl); 'when I had to go to hospital, they came round and were really friendly, did jokes and made me laugh' (11-year-old boy); 'when other people were calling me names, they used to encourage me to stand up, just to help me through" (11-year-old boy); 'when I've fallen, others stayed with me and tried to keep me calm, as I was upset' (11-year-old girl); 'when I was sick, my friend stayed with me, even though she was missing her favourite lesson, she kept talking to me, making me feel happy about it' (11-year-old boy). In their explanations, too, these children addressed the importance of such traits as empathy ('maybe they just felt sorry for me'), and loyalty ('you can rely on them, depend on them'; 'because they didn't just forget me'; 'she gave up something she loves to do to look after a friend'). The special school children mentioned very few examples which could be categorised as *caring*. However, issues of friendship, loyalty and emotional support could also be found in their more limited accounts: 'they made me better, kissed me' (11-year-old boy); 'they kept bullying me and my friend stuck up for me' (14-year-old boy); 'because they are friends and cuddle me' (11-year-old boy).

Parents' accounts of children's prosocial behaviour

Just as children mentioned *caring* behaviours least often, so parents, of both mainstream and special school children, mentioned such behaviours most often. Some of the examples given by special school parents referred to protective behaviour ('Daniel has this habit of going off by himself, and some of the children come and tell me before it gets dangerous'), reflecting their concern for their child's disability. Emotional support also figured largely in their accounts – cheering up a child in hospital, comforting a boy after a bicycle accident, being kind and supportive after a family bereavement. Mainstream parents described a number of variations on this theme of psychological support, including protection ('there was bullying at school, and so they ganged up and one of them organised his mother to pick the others up from school'), loyalty ('my daughter plays with these two girls, and she fell out with one, who then told the other girl to stop being friends with my daughter, but this girl stuck up for my daughter and said "Don't tell me who to play with"'), comfort ('my daughter disturbed burglars, and was very upset about it; four of her pals came round that night with a poster to make up for the upset') and sensitivity ('he had a bit of psoriasis and he was embarrassed, but when he went to the hospital, they were asking him nicely about it, and how he got on').

Children's *inclusion* behaviours, befriending another child and making him or her part of a group, also figured highly among parental examples. Many special school parents mentioned their child receiving invitations to a friend's house, for a party, for tea, or simply to play; and having someone to play with, who would 'treat her like a normal child, like one of the crowd' or 'younger children who . . . treat him like an older brother', was also a feature of their examples. These themes were largely absent from mainstream parents' examples of inclusion, which were more concerned with preventing isolation by 'not leaving someone out' and keeping someone company – 'if a child is sitting alone, going up to her and playing with her', and befriending – 'my daughter befriended this wee girl who was having a hard time from other girls'.

Parents' views of children's *helping* behaviour focused mainly on giving assistance to another child after an accident. There were stories about children cutting their knees, being bitten by a dog, and falling from bicycles (not all at the same time). The only few deviations from this theme came from mainstream parents, who also recalled children helping each other with schoolwork or domestic chores, or giving assistance to a child with a disability. Examples of *sharing* were rarely mentioned by either group of parents; mainstream parents' examples were exclusively limited to situations in which their child had forgotten either a lunch box or lunch money, and another child shared lunch or lent lunch money; the single example from a special school parent concerned her son receiving a present from a classmate. One may speculate that *sharing* behaviours are not highly valued by parents, with some justification as we shall see when we consider how adults respond to children's prosocial behaviours.

To a large extent, differences between the examples given by the two sets of parents, and the lack of variation in the special school parents' examples, can be explained by their different domestic experiences. The mainstream children in our sample lived at home with their parents, and in the same neighbourhood as their friends and schoolmates; there would therefore be ample opportunity for these parents to become familiar with their children's social interactions. The special school children, on the other hand, were normally bussed to school from different parts of the district. In this situation, the parents may have had little opportunity to observe their children interacting with peers from school.

Perhaps, in conclusion, it is worth quoting one well-articulated view of children's prosocial behaviour, provided by a mainstream parent:

> Basically, I think that nice behaviour is related to incidents where children will do things for unselfish reasons, for motivations which are not going to gratify themselves in the longer term. That cuts down the number of incidences to a bare minimum because I tend to believe children act in a selfish, egocentric way. It isn't just plain unselfish, there is a self-gratification attached to having a group within which one feels happy and content. The nice behaviour is suspect, something I find very difficult to define amongst children, particularly boys. *I find it difficult to observe genuinely nice behaviour in boys.* (Authors' italics).

Whether we agree with such a view or not, and all of us may feel that way on some days, it reminds us of the difficulties of interpreting children's prosocial behaviour, and of the challenge which faces us if we wish to promote such behaviour.

Teachers' accounts of children's prosocial behaviour

While children predominantly recounted examples of *inclusion*, and most of the parents' examples concerned *caring* or *inclusion*, teachers focused almost entirely on examples of *helping* and *caring* behaviours. The teachers' emphasis on *helping* is readily understandable in the context of their experience of children within the classroom. The mainstream teachers exclusively mentioned children helping each other with schoolwork, often in the context of a child with learning difficulties: 'if a child has been off ill, other children will help them to catch up with the work'; 'one wee girl was having difficulty with the work to the extent that she was upset coming to school, and another girl decided to take her under her wing and they worked really well together'; 'a pupil came to school with severe learning difficulties, and I was struck how supportive the others were of this boy, checking he knew what to do'. Teachers in special schools also referred to children helping each other with classwork, and to children giving assistance after an accident ('somebody fell and another boy pulled him in to me for a plaster'), but the majority of their examples reflected the children's concern with each other's physical difficulties: 'the more able will assist the less able without being asked – collect cushions, jackets'; 'where one child helps another do something perhaps they couldn't do, like putting on their shoes or coat'.

Teachers' examples of *caring* included the same variations on psychological support as were mentioned by the parents. There were examples of sensitivity ('they help her without making a fuss, so nobody knows she's getting help and she doesn't feel bad about it'; 'a child fell and was embarrassed and another child went up and told him not to worry'); comfort ('on a school trip, one child was upset about being away and got great sympathy from the others'; 'one child had been hit on the face, and Brian went to the sink and dipped the towel in water and bathed her face and washed away her tears'); protection ('if a child is being bullied, they rally round, protect that child and come and report it'); and a mainstream teacher's somewhat cynical version of loyalty ('they are quick enough to help one another if you are dealing with one; they are good witnesses, willing to lie for each other, back each other up, cover up for each other').

Where different emphasis has been given by the different groups to different types of prosocial behaviours, this may plausibly be explained either by their different attitudes and expectations about which child behaviours matter, and therefore which child behaviours they take note of, or in terms of the behaviours which are most relevant to their own interactions with children. For example, special school teachers reported many examples of children giving each other physical assistance, with shoes, trays, etc., which presumably reflected their experience of the needs of the children in their care. To the extent that such different emphases do reflect different expectations and attitudes, it is likely that this will have an influence on the way that adults respond to children's social behaviours. When a child behaves prosocially, what, if any, feedback and encouragement does she receive?

In a further study, we tried to find an answer to this question by presenting children, parents and teachers with pictorial examples of a child behaving prosocially towards another child, and asking them what they would do if they saw a child behaving like this. The pictures depicted a variety of examples of *sharing, helping, caring* and *inclusion* behaviours, and we gathered around 350 responses from each group.

Responding to children's prosocial behaviours

What would you do if you witnessed a child lending lunch money to another child? or helping a child who has fallen and cut his knee? or inviting a friend home for tea? or supporting another child who is getting into trouble? Would you let them get on with it? Or would you try to intervene by giving advice or a warning? Would you deliberately keep an eye on events to ensure that all went well? Would you draw other children's attention to this as an example of good behaviour, and talk about it? Or would you quietly congratulate the child? All such reactions were proposed by the children, parents and teachers in our study, but with some interesting differences.

Both children and their parents were most likely to say they would 'do nothing' if they saw a child behaving well (50% and 44% of responses respectively); even teachers were quite likely to see no need for action (19% of responses). Good behaviour is, of course, neither a problem nor a threat to the *status quo*, and so it doesn't require a response, a point made by many adults ('I wouldn't need to do anything there'). A small but significant number of responses, particularly from adults but also from children, were attempts to inhibit the behaviour, because of its implications: for example, 'don't lend money because you might have trouble getting it back', 'don't invite someone home to your house unless you've checked with your mother first', 'don't help him with his classwork – that's my job'. While these may all be perfectly sensible responses, based upon experience, they are hardly designed to encourage the behaviour or to commend the actor. There were two types of response that were particularly characteristic of teachers, and demonstrated their professional sense of responsibility to the children. The first might be called a 'contingent response', and involved monitoring the situation, finding out more about the background to the interaction before deciding whether to act; and the second explicitly used the target behaviour for the purposes of education ('we'd talk about that in class', 'I'd point out to the others that they should be doing that as well'). The only responses which could be seen as unreservedly positive and encouraging were those involving participation ('I would sit beside him too', 'I would say – can I help?') and verbal encouragement ('I would say – that's nice, well done'). Parents offered a limited number of both responses in equal measure (10%), while children were much more likely to suggest participation (21% of responses), and it was mainly left to teachers to offer verbal encouragement (25%).

Of course, all responses are situation specific, and depend upon the personalities of the players and the context of the interaction. Decisions about whether and how to respond depend upon an assessment of what is appropriate and what would be acceptable to the parties involved. Nonetheless, many of the responses proposed above suggest that children's prosocial behaviour is not given a great deal of encouragement. Adults are prone to ignore good behaviour, take over a child's attempts, warn of potential difficulties ahead, or embarrass the child with public recognition. Which raises the question – how then can we encourage prosocial behaviour? The approach which we are proposing in this book is to help children to understand and to articulate the motivations for, and consequences of both prosocial and antisocial behaviours, by means of peer discussions.

1. Focus your attention on examples of child prosocial behaviours that you have witnessed, and clarify what you identify as 'good' behaviour. Do your best examples differ from those described in the preceding sections?
2. Attempt to describe the context in which prosocial behaviour occurs, with reference to its precursors (what led to the behaviour?), its motivations (why did the child decide to behave like that?), and its consequences (how was the behaviour received by its recipient? What feedback, if any, did the child receive for behaving in this way?). What part did you play in the interaction?
3. Attempt your own taxonomy of children's prosocial behaviours.
4. Reflect upon your own responses to children behaving well. Are you someone who cautiously warns of the pitfalls, who enthusiastically praises, or who lets things take their course without interference or encouragement? What influences your choice of response?

As we shall see in succeeding chapters, our basic premiss is that it is important to get children talking about good behaviour, and a useful exercise to start this process off is to get them to think of and describe their own examples of such behaviour. Depending upon their expertise, this can be done as a written exercise, or they could draw their examples in a picture story. One way to encourage children to think about their own experiences is to work in pairs or in small groups.

1. Interviews: Rather as if they are interviewing each other for a newspaper or radio/television news programme, children can enjoy narrating their experiences of other people behaving well, in ways that made them feel good.
2. Behaviour Oscars: Groups of children can act as an Oscar Committee, and debate nominees for the day's/week's prosocial Oscar. Nominees and justifications can then be debated in class and voted upon.

Chapter 4

Children's Antisocial Behaviour

If prosocial behaviours are defined as those in which an individual uses his or her resources to achieve positive outcomes for someone else, then we might define antisocial behaviours as those in which an individual attempts to cause negative outcomes, either physical or psychological, for another person or persons. One might say that, while the underlying emotion in prosocial behaviour is empathy, the relevant emotions in antisocial behaviour are anger and hostility. Just as there is a wide range of different forms of children's prosocial behaviour through which empathy might be expressed, there are also many different types of behaviour which might be described as antisocial in which anger, hostility or aggression are latent or manifest. To begin with, let us consider two recent, very different examples of behavioural episodes which might be described as antisocial.

The first example is of extreme violence directed by a group of children against an individual in a public place. The incident took place in broad daylight beside a fairly busy road in a relatively affluent residential area of one of Britain's major cities. The victim was a 12-year-old boy who was skating on the pavement wearing roller blades. The attackers were a group of four boys who were a little older and physically larger than the victim. They used as a weapon an aerosol canister of lighter fuel which they ignited and directed at the victim's roller blades. The boy's boots and parts of his clothing were engulfed in flames as the attackers made their escape leaving the victim writhing in pain and extreme distress on the pavement. To any objective observer this was an horrific attack; it was deliberate, probably premeditated and clearly intended to harm the victim in a most callous way. Disturbingly, the attack was carried out in full view of several motorists drawing up at an adjacent set of traffic lights. As the victim struggled to beat out the flames, no one came to his assistance – a telling example of the all-too-familiar phenomenon of 'bystander apathy'. Indeed, having somehow managed to smother the flames, the boy then had to make his painful way home on hands and knees, and still no one helped him. This reluctance to help someone clearly in distress, in other words this failure to act prosocially, is arguably another form of antisocial behaviour – in this instance a sin of 'omission', a lack of care, rather than of 'commission' – but antisocial, nevertheless.

The second episode occurred in a primary school classroom. It was not an isolated incident, but a pattern of behaviour which developed quite subtly over a period of time. The victim in this instance was a girl aged ten who was made to feel that a group of her former friends were ganging up on her by deliberately and consistently (in her eyes at least) ignoring and excluding her. When the victim had reason to ask to borrow something or had to ask the others about class work, she described the feeling of them looking straight through her, 'as if I were a ghost'. She was tormented, miserable, and felt both helpless and isolated, not being able to bring herself to tell anyone what was happening because she felt people would just think she was making a fuss about nothing. Clearly the group of children in this instance were behaving antisocially as far as the isolated child was concerned, but their behaviour either went unnoticed by the class teacher, or was seen, but not recognised as antisocial. Just as in the case of prosocial behaviours, therefore, there might be different perceptions of antisocial behaviour.

Let us examine the two situations described in a little more detail and consider whether there may be different perceptions or interpretations of the behaviours in question. In the case of the attack on the boy in the street, we clearly have an example of criminal violence – an instance of extremely antisocial behaviour. Nevertheless, it is conceivable that the attackers felt 'justified' in their actions by their view that the 'victim' was showing off on his roller blades and needed to be 'taught a lesson'. They might claim that they had never seriously intended to set the boots and clothing on fire and that when this happened, they simply panicked and ran off, fearing (correctly) that they would be in serious trouble if caught. Similarly one might also ask what interpretation the 'apathetic bystanders' in their cars could possibly have placed on the observed incident which could account for their failure to come to the child's aid. If they chose not to look too closely at what was happening, they may have interpreted the fracas as simply an example of youths engaging in a bit of 'rough and tumble' and perhaps even a bit of play-acting. Probably a more likely explanation of their apparent apathy would be the feeling of reluctance to get involved through fear of personal injury and hence a deliberate decision not to go to help even though they may have been quite well aware of what was happening.

In the classroom episode, the group of children may have felt that the victim was simply in the habit of being a nuisance and a distraction in class by not allowing them to get on with their work assignments. They were aware of the tactic of ignoring misbehaviour which the teacher herself openly espoused and they may collectively have decided that this would be the best way to discourage what they considered to be the victim's inappropriate behaviour. From the teacher's point of view, she may have been aware of the victim tending to seek reassurance and assistance from others in class, or that the victim might have been somewhat socially isolated for a period. She might even have been aware of the group in question showing what she felt were desirable work habits in that they spent a good deal of time 'on-task', not allowing themselves to be distracted. However, as far as the teacher was concerned, the situation may well have simply seemed unremarkable, as no complaints had been received from either side to draw her attention to what was really going on.

In this chapter we shall explore the kinds of behaviour which we feel can be described as antisocial and which might in turn be profitably discussed, explored and challenged by children in associated classroom activities. The label 'antisocial' can clearly be attached to all forms of violence involving children, including vandalism and breach of the peace, behaviours which, according to the recent Gulbenkian Foundation Report (1995), have increased in prevalence during the past ten years. It is also interesting that the Commission drew attention to the continuing presence in the UK of ambivalent attitudes towards violence, and cited the fact that violent punishments remain legally and socially acceptable. In this context, during the last year of the Conservative Government there were even calls from ministers for the reconsideration of corporal punishment in schools. While acknowledging the seriousness and significance of the more extreme forms of antisocial behaviour, the label 'antisocial' also properly applies to more subtle forms of behaviour. We shall concentrate our attention on these, focusing primarily on problems of interpersonal behaviour and peer relationships, such as bullying, which many children are likely to experience in schools, and which teachers have a responsibility to deal with in order to make children's time at school as safe as possible.

In the survey described in the last chapter, as well as eliciting examples of prosocial behaviour, we asked respondents to describe from their own experiences examples of mean or nasty behaviour. Children were asked to describe an incident in which another child had been mean to them or had done something to upset them. Teachers were asked to describe similar episodes which they had witnessed or had reported to them in their class, and parents described child behaviours which they had witnessed, or which their own child had reported having experienced or witnessed. Again at this point, readers might pause and try to recall their own experiences of children being mean or nasty. What kinds of examples come to mind? How, if at all, did you react towards the perpetrator of the mean or nasty behaviour?

A total of 250 examples of antisocial behaviour were elicited from the various groups (see Chapter 3), and content analysed to establish different categories of antisocial behaviour. The categories which emerged (*verbal abuse, physical abuse, rejection* and *delinquent behaviour*) were broadly similar to the categories identified in research on bullying (e.g. Whitney and Smith 1993) and are defined below in Table 4.1.

Table 4.1 Categories of antisocial behaviour and their definitions, from elicited descriptions

Category	Definition
Verbal abuse	Ridicule, threats, gestures, dirty looks
Physical abuse	Hitting, kicking, tripping, spitting, throwing things; intent to cause physical harm
Rejection	Ganging up on or excluding someone, ostracism; stealing friends; treating someone differently
Delinquency	Stealing, vandalism, extortion

As in the case of the prosocial behaviours, we cannot tell whether a particular example was recalled because it was a particularly striking or unusual occurrence or because it was a frequent experience. Nevertheless we might look to see whether there are any noteworthy differences among the various subject groups in terms of the categories of antisocial behaviour they tended to recall. These differences are briefly summarised in Table 4.2 and will be discussed in more detail in the subsequent sections.

Table 4.2 Percentage of examples of each antisocial category provided by each subject group.

	Children		Parents		Teachers	
Category	Mainstream	Special	Mainstream	Special	Mainstream	Special
Verbal	50	18	35	48	52	28
Physical	28	74	35	24	26	38
Rejection	17	4	21	24	20	19
Delinquent	5	4	9	5	2	16

The table shows that for children and teachers in mainstream schools, *verbal abuse* was the most frequently mentioned type of behaviour, followed by *physical abuse*. On the other hand in the special schools this pattern was reversed with both children and teachers, but not parents, more likely to describe examples of *physical abuse*; this prevalence of examples of *physical abuse* was particularly marked in the sample of special school children. Other points worth noting are that examples of *rejection* were rarely elicited from special school children; and that while behaviours categorised as *delinquent* were relatively rare, children and teachers in special schools were more likely to describe such behaviours than were their mainstream counterparts.

Children in mainstream schools, when asked to give an example of another child being mean or nasty, most frequently described instances of *verbal abuse*. Examples of this category included being ridiculed or made fun of, either for some shortcoming, such as being

Children's accounts of antisocial behaviour

useless at football or not knowing the answer in class, or because of some physical characteristic like being overweight, wearing glasses or being small in stature: 'because I am quite small for my age, people were saying "midget" and stuff like that' (14-year-old boy). Many of the children, when describing instances of verbal abuse, commented in such a way as to suggest that they were aware of the possible motivation: 'it's unfriendly, they want you to start a fight or something so you get into trouble' (12-year-old boy); 'they just want to look good in front of their pals' (13-year-old girl). Some children attributed the behaviour to jealousy, as in the cases of children accused of being 'teacher's pet' or being called a 'swot' because they had done well in a class test. There were a few particularly unpleasant examples of hurtful verbal abuse: 'making fun of me when my dad died' (12-year-old girl). There were also examples which referred to rather non-specific name-calling: 'just name-calling really, and contradicting everything I say, trying to make it bad' (12-year-old boy). The latter type of example was most evident among the descriptions of verbal abuse given by the children from the special schools: 'they called me names and that – they just called me names' (13-year-old girl).

Examples of *physical abuse* were described by 28% of mainstream pupils and no fewer than 74% of children from the special schools. Children's examples in this category ranged from the relatively innocuous, 'this girl was pushing me around' (14-year-old girl), to more serious personal attacks. Rather disturbingly some of the latter took place in the school playground and in corridors or stairways, as illustrated in the following examples from a secondary school: 'several people got their noses broken earlier this year by the kids from the housing scheme – they act all hard and push people around' (14-year-old boy); 'I was pushed and fell right down the whole flight of stairs' (13-year-old girl). Another child described the kind of incident which takes place where discipline is not maintained at times when children are moving round the school: 'when the teacher is late for class and there is another class waiting, quite often they make fun of me – they punch me and laugh at me' (13-year-old boy). The same child went on to explain, 'they know they are quite strong, they know they can inflict pain, but don't realise just how hurtful it can be; they don't think about it'. Another secondary pupil recalled an incident from his days in primary school: 'there was quite a lot of them, it was snowing and they all got me on the ground and put snow all over my face' (14-year-old boy).

As noted above, three-quarters of all examples of antisocial behaviour described by children in special schools were in the category *physical abuse*. Many of these descriptions were rather terse and relatively unspecific, although some were quite lurid: 'he kicked me' (9-year-old boy); 'they battered me, punching and kicking me' (13-year-old boy); 'we were playing and they burst my nose' (9-year-old boy). While many of the incidents clearly took place outside in the school grounds, there were some which took place inside special school buildings, such as the example provided by one 12-year-old girl: 'two girls and a boy were bad to me; one girl punched me in the back and the boy punched me as well when we were at music today'. For some of the children, the antisocial behaviour they had experienced was evidently part of a transaction in which they were participating in one way or another: 'he came up and annoyed me; he was hitting me and I hit him back' (9-year-old girl).

Roughly one sixth of the examples given by children in the mainstream schools, but a much smaller proportion of those from special schools, described behaviour which could be categorised as *rejection*. One 14-year-old girl simply referred to children 'being horrible to other people, not sitting next to them and upsetting them'. Sometimes it was clearly the behaviour of a group of children deliberately 'ganging up' on an individual, as in the example cited at the beginning of the chapter of the child being made to feel like a ghost by the group collectively ignoring her. Other examples involved upsetting fickleness on the part of former friends: 'When I was in primary school, I had two really good friends, but it went wrong and we fell out and they ended up ganging up against me. They would talk about things they had done together in front of me when they knew I hadn't' (13-year-old girl). The same girl went on to explain: 'Maybe it was just a phase they were going through, or maybe they had just agreed not to like me. I don't really know'. Another girl described the process of friendships being broken in the following way: 'Well, someone tried to steal my friends. I used to be this person's friend and we had a big argument and then she started becoming really pally with my other friends even though she didn't really like them before' (11-year-old girl). There were also examples of an individual child deliberately excluding or isolating another as in the example described by a 12-year-old boy: 'I was out cycling with a friend and stopped for a minute to tie my shoelace and my friend did not stop, just kept going. I tried to catch up with him but he was nowhere in sight'. The examples of this kind of antisocial behaviour given by special school children were less detailed but no less poignant: 'I was in my pal's house and they left me; they just left me on my own' (10-year-old girl).

A few children described more 'serious' forms of antisocial behaviour which were categorised as *delinquent*. While these examples were relatively rare, they were undoubtedly disturbing, including violent personal attacks, damage to property and threatening behaviour. As an illustration, one 11-year-old boy related the following: 'When I was walking down the road with my pal I was hit in the face with a brick'. He went on to explain: 'They were from another area. They just wanted to pick a fight with people from my area'. It was perhaps worth noting that none of the examples of delinquent behaviour were described by girls.

*Parents' accounts
of antisocial
behaviour*

As with the children, most of the examples of antisocial behaviour provided by parents fell into the categories of *verbal* and *physical abuse*. The thoughtlessness and hurtfulness of some children was clearly evident in the way some of the parents described cruel examples of verbal abuse to which their children had been subjected: 'After my son had an operation on his mouth, some other kids were upsetting him by slagging him off – they were laughing at him because his teeth came out and the others were just coming through' (female parent of primary pupil). The frequent examples of verbal abuse described by parents of special school children showed how much this kind of behaviour was part of their children's social experience: 'My daughter gets picked on because she is a bit different, you know. Occasionally she'll get pushed or something like that, but mostly it's just name-calling' (female parent of special school pupil). Accounts like this might seem to indicate a degree of acceptance, or that name-calling is somehow less 'serious' than other forms of antisocial behaviour. However, there is no questioning the level of unpleasantness associated with examples like the following in which a child's particular needs or lack of understanding of situations appeared to be a stimulus to the perpetrators. 'Last year before my child came to this school, she had an awful time with one particular child making hurtful comments. This child had picked up on the fact that my child has a problem with toileting. She gave her a dreadful time shouting things at her in the playground' (female parent of special school pupil); 'my son came home one day very upset; he had been told by another child that his sister had been killed' (male parent of special school pupil).

Parents were clearly very much aware of and disturbed by the verbal abuse directed at their children when they were away from the special schools, for example, when playing at home or out shopping, even where, as in the following example, the child who was the target of the abuse was not fully aware of it: 'Somebody ... talking about my daughter and her not really hearing it. Like "there's one of them mongol weans, them spastic weans"' (female parent of special school pupil).

Parents often recounted incidents involving *physical abuse* which had taken place either in or out of school. Interestingly, while special school children themselves most often described examples of physical abuse, special school parents were relatively less likely to give examples in this category than were their children or mainstream parents. As noted in the last chapter this could be due to the fact that the children were typically bussed to their special school which was geographically separated from home, making it less likely that the parents would be directly aware of such incidents taking place. One secondary school parent made explicit reference to physical proximity to the school in her account: 'overlooking the playground, you can see incidents where children are pushing and shoving one another'. Perhaps children in the mainstream schools were simply more likely to report any incidents of physical abuse to their parents than were those in special schools. The range of behaviours described by parents in the category of physical abuse was similar to the range described by pupils, and parents' accounts also varied in their specificity. Some were rather general in nature, referring presumably to a series of incidents: 'when my youngest child first started school, he was physically bullied; he was punched and kicked by a certain boy' (male parent of primary pupil). Others more clearly described a specific incident: 'one incident was in the swimming pool where this girl was pushing my daughter down in the water, which frightened her a lot' (female parent of primary pupil).

Several parents both in mainstream and special schools gave accounts of examples of social *rejection*. A typical example from a primary school parent was: 'coming back to school after a school trip some of my daughter's friends formed their own clique and she was told she wasn't part of it and they wouldn't speak to her'. However it was not just parents of girls who described examples of rejection: 'my son was quite hurt because a friend of his wouldn't let him play football saying, "who said you could play?" and saying to other children, "he's terrible at football, he's a clown at football." '. In the latter example it was one child who was actively seeking to exclude another; in the former it was more clearly the collective action of a group against an individual child. There were also examples where there was no explicit reference to *intent* to exclude, but where, nevertheless the victim had suffered: '(she) was having a hard time from the other children because she was new – it was mainly them just not involving her in their activities' (male secondary parent). In the examples provided by special school parents there was evidence, just as in the case of physical abuse, that the nature of the child's special needs may have been seen as the 'reason' why the child was victimised: 'My son wants to play football but doesn't really know how to play and the other children get irritated with him because they want the game to run properly. It usually ends up with my son coming home upset because he has not been allowed to join in' (male special school parent).

A few parents described rather more serious forms of antisocial behaviour which were categorised as *delinquent*. These included theft, extortion, damage to property and serious assaults: 'My son was seriously assaulted in the street by members of a gang' (male secondary parent). While the majority of examples in this category took place outside of school, there were some which took place in school and although arguably less serious, clearly involved deliberate damage to property: 'Some kids were damaging my kid's stuff, breaking pencils and things' (female primary parent).

Teachers' accounts of antisocial behaviour

As with both parents and children, teachers most frequently described examples in the two categories, *verbal abuse* and *physical abuse*. Mainstream teachers were twice as likely to give examples of verbal abuse than physical abuse. Special school teachers, on the other hand, were more likely to describe physical than verbal abuse.

In the *verbal abuse* category, the potential seriousness of this kind of behaviour was reflected in several examples from both mainstream and special schools: 'One boy with social problems was constantly being made fun of and being picked on – mainly verbal abuse, but it got so bad that his parents withdrew him from the school' (male secondary teacher). 'One child had been made a fool of by others who were saying particularly nasty things about (his) home and family which hurt' (female special school teacher). The potential consequences in terms of damaged self-esteem was explicitly or implicitly referred to by some teachers in their accounts of verbal abuse: 'One boy was picking on another making him feel bad about himself by saying things like, "You're a tramp, look at those trainers, why don't you wear any decent gear?"' (male primary teacher). According to teachers' accounts, therefore, children with special educational needs were the victims of verbal abuse, but this was not only confined to the children in special schools. For example, more than one mainstream primary teacher described children with special educational needs being deliberately 'wound up' by other children mocking their learning difficulties.

Under the heading of *physical abuse* teachers gave examples of a wide range of antisocial actions perpetrated by individuals and by groups, by boys and by girls. Several quite disturbing incidents, or series of incidents, were described, such as the following secondary teacher's account:

> One group picking on a child with special educational needs actually spat on him and tried to trip him up. This happened at interval time in the corridors at the change of class and most noticeably in the lunch hour in the playground. When the snow was on the ground he was pelted with snowballs. Because of his slight disability and small stature and because of his nature, because he wasn't able to retaliate, he became a victim.

One might legitimately ask what the school was doing about such a situation. The teacher in question commented at some length about how difficult it was for the school to deal with the antisocial behaviour involved in this particular episode. Readers may wish to consider at this point whether it would be possible for such a situation to develop in the school with which they are most closely involved and, if so, what they would wish to see done to deal with, or to prevent, the behaviour in question.

The examples of physical abuse provided by special school teachers included instances of behaviour which was to an extent uncontrolled rather than deliberate and wilful: 'One child just physically kicks out aggressively, so much so that the other children are very frightened of him' (female special school teacher). 'One particular child will scratch other children or nip them, if he doesn't like what they are doing' (female special school teacher). 'One child suddenly got up and attacked another child, trying to strangle him. When the other children went to the child's defence, he turned and bashed one of them then ran out of the room' (female special school teacher). However, many examples of deliberately hurtful behaviour were also reported: 'One child gathered a group together and picked on others. There was pushing and shoving and a bit of nipping'. 'One child in the class has very cruel tendencies and picks on a child with spina bifida who has two sticks. He might deliberately kick the sticks away from the child or try to trip him up, kicking his feet away' (female special school teacher).

Even though they might be expected to be less visible in the classroom, examples of *rejection* were given by some of the teachers. Teachers showed in the way they described these examples that they were aware of the potential consequences for the victims of rejection: 'When two, three or four children gang up together and harass another pupil making statements such as, "We're all in this together and you're not one of the group", this makes the child feel isolated, unwanted and inadequate' (male special school teacher). Both boys and girls were identified as victims in these accounts, typically the boys being excluded from some specific activity (usually a game of football) and the girls falling foul of splits in friendship groups.

Among the teachers' accounts there were only a few examples in the final category of *delinquent* behaviour. However, one particularly disturbing example from a special school was described which graphically illustrates the kind of challenge which on occasion teachers may find they have to face: 'one child recently took a hearing aid from another child, took the battery out of it and threw it away so that the child could no longer hear'.

One thing to note about the accounts of antisocial behaviour given by children, parents and teachers is that there was a considerable degree of correspondence in the range and types of behaviours described among the three groups, certainly a greater degree of correspondence than was evident when we considered prosocial behaviour. It is important to ask whether this greater consistency among groups extended to the ways in which individuals tend to respond to such behaviours or deal with the kinds of situations involved. This is certainly a very relevant question for schools to consider when, for example, they are trying to develop an effective anti-bullying policy.

Responding to children's antisocial behaviour

In our survey the most frequent category of proposed response to 'bad' or antisocial behaviour, particularly by children and parents, was to stop the behaviour by verbal means. Children and parents also frequently suggested they would report the behaviour to someone in authority. Teachers, on the other hand, were more likely to adopt positive strategies and attempt to elicit a change in the behaviour of the perpetrator, for example, by encouraging role reversal. In cases of physical and verbal abuse, teachers were more likely than parents or other children to say they would stop the behaviours by verbal means. In their responses to rejection behaviours, it was teachers who indicated they would investigate the circumstances and offer advice to the victim.

In sharp contrast to their frequent unresponsiveness to prosocial behaviour, adults, and particularly teachers, almost always indicated they would take action to deal with instances of antisocial behaviour. Teachers, reflecting their professional duty of care, indicated a range of strategies which they would adopt. They claimed that they would take responsibility in the situation, seek to 'educate' the children involved wherever possible, and take constructive steps to promote good behaviour and replace the bad. In this respect, the teachers differed from the parents and the children who were more likely to pass responsibility for action to some figure of authority in the school rather than seek to deal with the behaviour themselves. One might ask whether this tendency to pass on responsibility is perhaps another manifestation of the kind of bystander apathy which concerned us at the beginning of the chapter? Much of the unpleasant, antisocial behaviour experienced by children took place in the playground where there were likely to be many other children present who could have taken more assertive action in support of the victim. As recent anti-bullying packages have argued (McLean 1994), a central issue for schools is how to encourage a more proactive bystander community, in which all will participate in the promotion of prosocial behaviour.

Parent/teacher activities

1. Focus on any examples you might encounter of children's antisocial behaviour. Try to pinpoint what it is that you find unacceptable about the behaviour in question. What, essentially, makes the behaviour antisocial? Can you perhaps form a working definition of antisocial behaviour? You might also consider whether the kinds of examples you identify are different from those described above. For each of a few chosen examples, try to describe in as much detail as you can the context in which it occurred, its antecedents (what prompted the behaviour?), what motivated the behaviour (why did the child behave like that?) and its consequences (how did the victim respond and what response, if any, was there to the behaviour on the part of others, including yourself?; what was done to stop the behaviour or what sanctions were applied to the perpetrator?).
2. Try to map out your own set of categories of antisocial behaviour.
3. Reflect on and evaluate your present strategies for dealing with antisocial behaviour. This is best done as part of a small working group and the process of evaluation will, of course, benefit from the involvement of children and parents.

There is much to be gained from providing opportunities for children to talk about interpersonal behaviour, both desired, appropriate, prosocial behaviour and undesirable, inappropriate, antisocial behaviour. As we suggested for prosocial behaviour, probably the best place to start is by asking children to think of and describe their own examples of antisocial behaviour. For older children this can take the form of a written exercise, or alternatively children might attempt to represent the behaviour by means of a single drawing or a picture story. The value of such activity can be enhanced where children work collaboratively in pairs or in a small group.

Classroom activities

1. Pairs: Children might interview one another and take turns as reporter/interviewer and victim respectively to produce items for a newspaper or radio/television news report.
2. Groups: Each group member can narrate an example of antisocial behaviour which they have experienced, and which the group could then discuss, categorise and make recommendations about appropriate responses.

Chapter 5

Improving Children's Social Awareness and Behaviour

As we have indicated on a number of occasions, our central concerns in this book are the development of children's socio-moral awareness, and the importance of taking positive steps to foster children's prosocial behaviour. We wish to promote 'social behaviour' as a topic for learning, discussion and understanding in the classroom. Although the relationship between knowledge and action is never simple and direct, nonetheless it is a basic tenet of education that by developing understanding we can influence behaviour. By focusing children's attention on the nature and significance of their social interactions, therefore, our aim is to encourage them towards more positive social behaviour. It bears repeating that this approach involves a change of emphasis from more reactive educational strategies which focus upon the inhibition of antisocial behaviours, towards proactive support for prosocial behaviours. As some of the adult responses described in Chapter 3 have demonstrated, it is all too easy to take children's prosocial behaviours for granted. Of course, a considerable amount of child management, both in the classroom and in the home, involves the maintenance of order, but this does not mean that prosocial child behaviours, because they are non-disruptive, can be ignored.

In Chapter 1 we discussed the skills and attributes which contribute to prosocial behaviours, such as recognising and responding to other perspectives, other minds; the capacity to communicate one's own thoughts and feelings; being able to exhibit empathy and concern for others; an awareness of the rules of social interaction, including, most importantly, moral rules and a consideration for others' welfare. These skills go hand in hand with the development of friendships and positive interpersonal relations, and as such, should be central to our attempts to educate for prosocial behaviour. In this chapter, we will consider how the aim of fostering children's prosocial interactions can be translated into practice, by means of a series of classroom tasks and activities which are designed to develop the above skills.

One of the most encouraging developments in recent years has been the educational benefit which children can gain from collaborative work, from sharing ideas and developing understanding through peer discussions. Such an approach has a strong theoretical basis, and has found considerable support from empirical research. Despite its critics and potential difficulties, group work in the classroom is neither an educational gimmick nor a means of optimising teacher contact time, and peer tutoring, group discussions and collaborations now play a prominent role at all levels of education.

The process of learning is essentially the modification of the framework of our knowledge in the presence of new or conflicting information. We learn to master concepts, to solve problems, and to achieve better understandings through a consideration of such new information, in the light of which we can recognise the inadequacy of our previous perceptions and understanding. Three of the most influential theorists of children's learning and cognitive development have been Jean Piaget, Lev Vygotski and Jerome Bruner, whose complementary views on the learning process underlie our present approach. In Piagetian terms, learning occurs when we experience a state of mental disequilibrium in which our current understanding conflicts with new evidence. Whether children are learning about scientific concepts such as the causes of floating and sinking, societal concepts such as the role of government and taxation, or socio-moral concepts such as the appropriate administration of justice, properly managed peer discussions, in which conflicting views are expressed, have been found to enhance their learning and understanding. Vygotski discussed children's learning with reference to what he called a zone of proximal development, which can be defined as the cognitive distance between a child's current performance level and the level which she could achieve with assistance. The crux of Vygotski's argument is that children *learn through collaboration* with more competent others, be they peers or adults, and that conceptual understanding develops by a process of joint construction. Bruner likewise focuses upon the collaborative nature of learning, which he represents in terms of a scaffolding process, in which the 'teacher' provides the necessary framework or scaffold to help the child to better understanding. Excellent summaries of these theoretical perspectives can be found in, for example, Smith and Cowie (1991), and Garton and Pratt (1998).

The optimisation of children's learning through peer interactions appears to depend upon certain conditions: firstly, group discussions and negotiations should engage the participants' individual prior expertise and experience; secondly, levels of understanding within the group should also differ, so that conflicts do emerge in the discussion; and thirdly, learning should be supported by a task framework which helps learners to resolve challenges to their understanding. This last condition can be achieved, for example, by guided decision making and expert feedback. A further benefit of group collaborations, of particular relevance to the development of prosocial skills, is that they are participatory; thus, by joining in and articulating their thoughts and feelings, children are, *ipso facto*, developing their communication and interpersonal skills, at the same time as they are clarifying their own attitudes, ideas and understanding. Children are too often ill-equipped to talk about interpersonal matters, and the lack of such a skill can best be remedied by making the activity more familiar and commonplace.

Let us therefore now consider, in outline, the kind of classroom tasks appropriate to the aims we have described; more specific task details will be presented in Chapters 6 and 7. In Chapters 3 and 4 we discussed examples of prosocial and antisocial child behaviours which had been described by children and by adults, deriving from their own experiences. These examples have been translated into the cartoon-style drawings reproduced in this book, for use in the tasks. We have retained the four broad categories of prosocial behaviours – *caring, sharing, helping* and *inclusion* – and antisocial behaviours – *verbal abuse, physical abuse, rejection* and *delinquency* – which were previously discussed. The situations depicted in these picture stories have been selected for their representativeness, and all children should be able to easily relate them to their own interpersonal experiences. However, there is nothing sacrosanct about either this particular set of examples, or the behaviour categories which they represent, and we would also encourage the development of new categories and examples, if they seem more directly relevant to children in a given classroom. The important feature of the tasks is the thinking and discussion which they provoke.

One of the first requirements of our tasks is that they do tap into children's own social experiences, as a means of focusing their attention on interpersonal behaviours. Using the cartoon situations in a variety of combinations, the different tasks will require children, both individually and in groups, to make comparative judgements about different social behaviours; to discuss and explain these judgements with each other, and in so doing, to consider the causes and consequences of both prosocial and antisocial behaviours; and to role play and adopt the perspective of the participants in these interactions, namely both the initiator and the recipient of the behaviour. The tasks are therefore designed with the following aims in mind:

1. To encourage children to make explicit their relative, and different values, and to provide a forum for the consideration of such differences, thereby helping children to clarify and develop their own values and moral thinking.
2. To help to raise the profile and status of interpersonal behaviours in both children's thinking and awareness, and in the curriculum.
3. To make discussions about feelings, emotional responses and interpersonal relationships more acceptable in the classroom and beyond, and to help children to develop the language skills necessary for such discussions.
4. To encourage the development of empathic responses (a) by

focusing awareness on the motives and feelings of children who behave well and children who behave badly, and also on the feelings of the recipients of such behaviours, (b) by giving consideration to the consequences of social behaviours, and (c) by developing children's role-playing skills in interpersonal contexts.

The eight drawings depicted on the next page will provide a brief, general introduction to the tasks. They include one example of each of the four prosocial and four antisocial behaviours, with variations in the gender of the actor and the recipient of the behaviour. Thus, there are drawings of a boy *physically abusing* another boy (Drawing A); a girl *verbally abusing* another girl (B); a *delinquent* boy extorting money from a girl (C); a girl *rejecting* a boy from her group of friends (D); a boy *sharing* his lunch with a girl (E); a boy *helping* another boy with classwork (F); a *caring* girl visiting a sick boy (G), and a girl *including* (*accepting*) another girl into her company (H). The full set of examples of the eight behaviour categories is shown in the Appendix, demonstrating many further permutations of both gender and situation.

The purposes to which the variety of drawings can be put can be considered under four broad headings:

1. Tasks which foster children's thinking about the rules of social behaviour

We want to help children to develop the habit of thinking about the social nature of their actions, and about the reasons why certain behaviours are acceptable and others unacceptable. To further this aim, children can be asked to make comparisons between different prosocial and antisocial behaviours, and to explain their judgements, using a variety of combinations of behaviours. Such comparisons will focus their attention, not only upon the different motives and consequences of social behaviours, but also, and more especially, upon the social and moral rules which govern them. Children's judgements can be sought about individual behaviours ('what's good and what's bad about someone doing that?'), or comparisons can be made between two, three or even four behaviours, depending upon the extent of the child's capacity for meaningful comparisons. For example, comparing drawings A and C, children may be asked to judge which of these boys is behaving more badly, and to explain why, or to explain the rules which are being violated. Again, comparing drawings E, F and H, children can explain which of these good behaviours are preferred, which one they would most welcome from a friend, and why? Depending upon the sophistication of the children, they can be led to a discussion of why good behaviours are important, and why bad behaviours are antisocial.

Four examples of antisocial behaviours

A Michael kicks Jon and makes him drop his drink.

B Ann has a bad leg and walks with crutches. Jane laughs at her and shouts to her friends, "Look at the wimp that walks with a limp".

C Dan makes Nina give him money to spend in the school shop.

D Rachel and her pals are playing tig. Rachel tells Ben that he can't play with them.

Four examples of prosocial behaviours

E Alison has forgotten her lunch, so Peter is sharing his lunch with her.

F Colin is stuck with his classwork. Billy tries to help him.

G David is in hospital because he is ill. Tina goes to visit him in hospital.

H Mia sees a new girl at the school gate and says, "Do you want to walk up the road with me?"

2. Tasks which encourage children's understanding of the motivations in social interaction

When asked how they would respond to a particular example of child social behaviour, the adults, particularly the teachers, in our samples often stated that their response would involve monitoring children's behaviours in order to discover possible reasons for the behaviour. Being aware of, and sensitive to such influences upon others' social behaviours is central to successful social interaction, and to the development of friendships. Focusing children's attention upon the motives and causes for both prosocial and antisocial behaviours therefore forms an important component of our tasks. For any given social behaviour, children's interpretations and causal understandings can be explored and prompted by means of such questions as – 'what do you think happened to make him/her do that?'; 'have you seen somebody doing that? – why do you think she/he did that?'; 'have you done that? – why did you?'; 'when would you do that?'.

3. Tasks which focus on interpersonal feelings and role reversal

The capacity for empathy, for the sharing of feelings and emotions, is perhaps the most important single ingredient of successful social interaction. Developing the skills to express one's own feelings, and to be aware of how others are feeling, are considerable achievements, which are insufficiently practised and encouraged. The normalisation of such activities can be helped by tasks which explicitly require the discussion of feelings and emotions. For example, the feelings of the two participants before and after an interaction such as that in drawing D can be discussed and explored in a variety of ways. Will the participants' feelings change as a result of the interaction, and in what way? Children, in pairs or groups, can physically role play or merely imagine an interaction, or perhaps remember themselves in such a situation. How did/would they feel as either the initiator or the recipient of an antisocial or prosocial act? Games to encourage the linguistic expression of emotions can include choosing adjectives to fit feelings in different situations.

4. Tasks which encourage children to think of the consequences of actions

Being aware of the consequences of, and taking responsibility for one's actions is another hallmark of socialisation. The potential consequences for the participants in each of the cartoon situations can be explored and discussed, either in terms of a narrative 'what happens next?' game, or by asking children to decide what the participants should do next; more personally, children can be asked to decide what they would do if they witnessed, or were the recipient of such an interaction, or indeed, what experience they have of such interactions and their consequences, to themselves or to others. Other avenues of exploration include asking children what different responses to a given behaviour they would expect from a parent, a teacher, a pal, a sibling, an older/younger child at school.

While all of the tasks which are outlined above and described in subsequent chapters can be conducted with individual children, we would encourage their use in group situations, so that children can share their experiences and understanding, and learn from each others' different perspectives. In order to maximise the effectiveness of group discussions, the following guidelines may be helpful:

1. Group size and composition

Where indicated, tasks can be successfully conducted in pairs, but groups should usually and ideally be of three or four children; if they are larger then some children will probably not participate in a discussion (although they can also benefit from a passive, if attentive role). Our experience suggests that single sex groups can promote the most fruitful discussions, insofar as mixed sex groups can be dominated by the majority sex. However, mixed sex grouping can be very constructive, and individual teachers will find the best combinations in their own classrooms.

2. Encouraging group discussions

Two factors are relevant here – the age of the children, and the presence in the group of differences of opinion and understanding. Before initiating a group discussion, it is important to maximise individual differences, and to preempt the children from taking the easy option of simply agreeing with each other without any discussion. Individual differences of opinion about social behaviours can more often be found in mixed sex than in same sex groups. Teachers may also find it productive, where appropriate, to vary the composition of potential bullies and victims in a group. Another effective means of encouraging differences is to require individual group members to commit themselves to an opinion beforehand in writing. Children can be asked to write, on prepared answer sheets, their own individual judgements about the relevant behaviour, which they must then subsequently explain and justify to the group. With regard to the age of the children, among older groups (10 years upwards) discussions can take on a life of their own, independent of much adult support, whereas younger children require a more structured format, with more guidance helping them to give simpler judgements and explanations. For each of the tasks, the relevant aims and outcomes, as well as their age appropriateness, will be described in the task instructions.

To conclude, the classroom tasks we describe will encourage children –

(a) to be aware of other perspectives in a prosocial or antisocial interaction;

(b) to develop the capacity to communicate social attitudes, emotional feelings and personal experiences;

(c) to consider the reasons for, and consequences of, others' behaviour, in terms of their needs, personal circumstances, or the rules (social and moral) of social interaction;

(d) to speculate and to role play in hypothetical discussions about behaviours;

(e) to make, explain and justify comparative moral judgements about different behaviours in terms of rules, motives, causes and consequences;

(f) to consider appropriate responses to both prosocial and antisocial behaviours.

Chapter 6

Classroom Activities to Increase Interpersonal Awareness

In this chapter we shall outline some specific suggestions for classroom activities based on the use of the cartoon examples briefly described in Chapter 5. These suggestions are based on our experience of using these materials in primary, secondary and special schools with children aged 9 to 14 years, and on the many helpful comments of teachers with an interest in this area of research and curriculum development. In Chapter 2, we noted the appearance of other resources designed to support classroom activity in the general area of PSD. We very much welcome the opportunities these various packages create for linkage with the resources outlined in this book. The suggestions which follow will allow particular emphasis to be placed on interpersonal behaviour and relationships, aspects of the curriculum for PSD which we feel have been relatively overlooked. The activities are outlined in terms of their *purposes*, approximate intended *age level* of the children, suggested *organisation* (e.g. group or individual), *materials* required, and *instructions* for the children. The activities described also include, where appropriate, suggestions for further *follow-up* activity. Of course, as suggestions, the 'instructions' will lend themselves to adaptation as appropriate for local circumstances and according to the educational needs and abilities of particular groups of children. Such adaptations, as discussed in the following paragraphs, may be in terms of the selection of stimulus pictures, the use of captions, the precise focus of the task and/or the format of the responses expected from the children.

Selecting stimulus pictures

The tasks can be adapted to suit particular groups of children by varying the selection of stimulus pictures, either in terms of the categories of behaviour depicted or the number of examples which teachers feel would be appropriate for children to consider. Thus, for example, in the first activity, older children could be asked to respond to each of the 32 different cartoon situations, whereas younger children may respond best to a much smaller number, say eight cartoons, one from each category. Selection may also be in terms of the **category** of behaviour depicted. Some teachers may wish to focus particularly on certain categories, or even just one category of behaviour, in order to reflect the special interest of the class and/or particular needs of the children. Because there are two parallel sets of cartoons, teachers also have the option to use either the cartoons showing boys interacting with boys, cartoons showing girls interacting with girls, or by using the selective subset, cartoons showing girls and boys interacting together.

The caption provided for each of the situations depicted in the set of cartoons has been kept as simple and readable as possible, while retaining the meaning of the original description on which the cartoon was based. Of course, teachers should feel free to modify or rewrite the captions should they feel that the originals are unsuitable for any reason. When working with children whose competence as readers is deemed not to be sufficient, teachers may wish to dispense with the captions altogether, and conduct the activities by providing oral commentary on the cartoons as well as oral instructions.

Use of cartoon captions

Children of different ages and abilities may be provided with a variety of formats in which to make their responses to the suggested tasks. In the first specimen response sheet (Figure 6.1), children can be given a response scale in which cartoon faces depict a range of emotions to record how the character in the stimulus picture, or they themselves, would feel in each particular situation. This method of recording is suitable for younger children (5–8 years). An open-ended invitation to write a few words describing how they think the character, or they themselves, would be feeling in the particular situation would be more appropriate for some older children. Alternatively, the task need not involve any written response, but rather be presented as a stimulus for oral discussion.

Selecting the appropriate response format

The following tasks can be presented in a variety of ways, using different combinations of drawings. You may wish to explore children's thinking about different examples of one type of behaviour, so you can ask children to compare the different examples of *helping*: or you may wish children to think about different categories of behaviour, so you can show them a set of drawings, with one example being taken from each different category.

In this activity children have the opportunity to consider the cartoon depictions of interpersonal behaviours and to try to think about (a) how the person 'at the receiving end' of the behaviour depicted in the cartoon would be likely to be feeling; (b) how the 'actor' might feel; and (c) how they themselves would feel in the position as actor or recipient. Through this activity children become more aware of their own feelings about relationships and, by thinking about what others might be feeling in both favourable and unfavourable situations, develop their ability to empathise with other people's feelings.

Activity 1 – Recognising feelings about interpersonal behaviour

Activity 1	**Recognising feelings about interpersonal behaviour**
Purposes	To orientate children towards thinking about interpersonal behaviours; to encourage children to express their feelings about prosocial and antisocial behaviours; to encourage children to empathise with others' feelings in interpersonal interactions.
Age/level	All age groups.
Organisation	Individual, small-group or whole-class activity.
Materials	Basic set of 32 cartoons (either male or female characters), photocopied for individual children or on transparencies for OHP. Different selections of sub-sets of cartoons can be made. For example, children might focus only on the categories of prosocial behaviour or only on antisocial behaviour. Response sheets – (a) graphic faces scale for 5–9 year olds (see Figure 6.1); (b) written comments for 10 years upwards; or (c) combination of both graphic scale and written comment (see Figure 6.2).
Instructions	For each cartoon, children consider (a) "How do you think [name of recipient/victim] feels?" and (b) "How would you feel if someone behaved like that towards you?" They may also be asked (c) "How do you think [name of actor] is feeling?" Children can respond using the graphic scale and/or by written/spoken comment.
Follow-up	*Group discussion.* Choose to focus on the feelings of either the victim/recipient or the actor. Children working in pairs or small groups of three or four, are instructed to compare and explain their individual ratings/comments; they should then identify and discuss similarities and differences in their ratings/comments, i.e. on which behaviours did they agree or disagree, and why? Then, focusing their attention on how they themselves would feel in the depicted situations, children can discuss the range of positive and negative feelings within the group in response to the cartoon behaviours.

Figure 6.1 Recognising feelings about interpersonal behaviour

Emma is a new girl at school. **Katie** is showing her the way to the dinner hall.

Q1. How do you think Emma felt when Katie helped her?

Q2. If someone helped you like that, how would you feel?

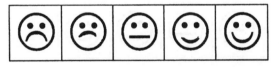

Q3. How do you think Katie was feeling when she helped Emma?

Q4. If you helped someone like that, how would you feel?

Figure 6.1 (cont.) Recognising feelings about interpersonal behaviour

Tom's family is poor and he wears shabby clothes. **George** sees Tom and shouts, "Tinky, tinky, your family are stinky".

Q1. How do you think Tom felt when George said nasty things about his family?

Q2. If someone said nasty things about your family like that, how would you feel?

Q3. How do you think George was feeling when he said nasty things to Tom?

Q4. If you ever said nasty things to someone like that, how would you feel?

Figure 6.2 Expressing feelings about interpersonal behaviour

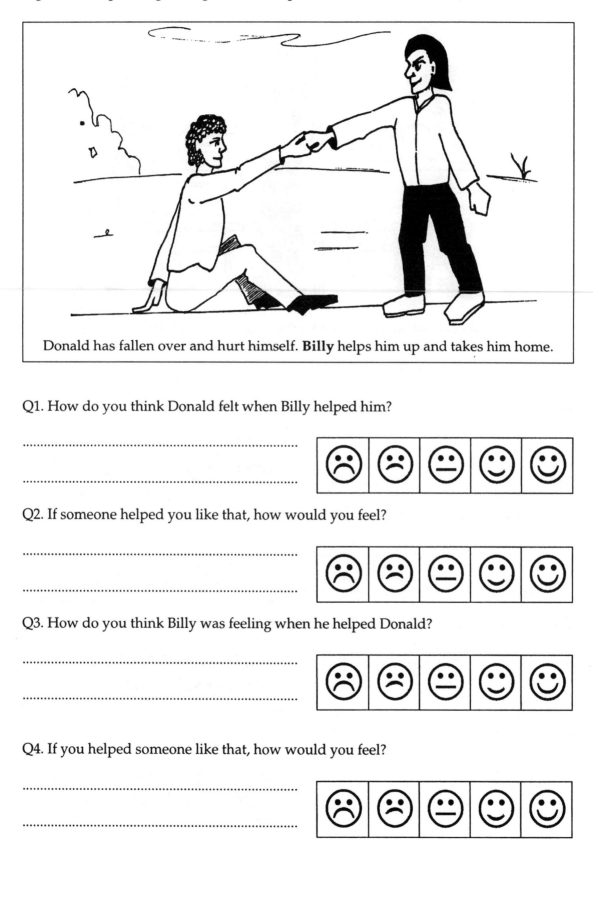

Donald has fallen over and hurt himself. **Billy** helps him up and takes him home.

Q1. How do you think Donald felt when Billy helped him?

....
....

Q2. If someone helped you like that, how would you feel?

....
....

Q3. How do you think Billy was feeling when he helped Donald?

....
....

Q4. If you helped someone like that, how would you feel?

....
....

Figure 6.2 (cont.) Expressing feelings about interpersonal behaviour

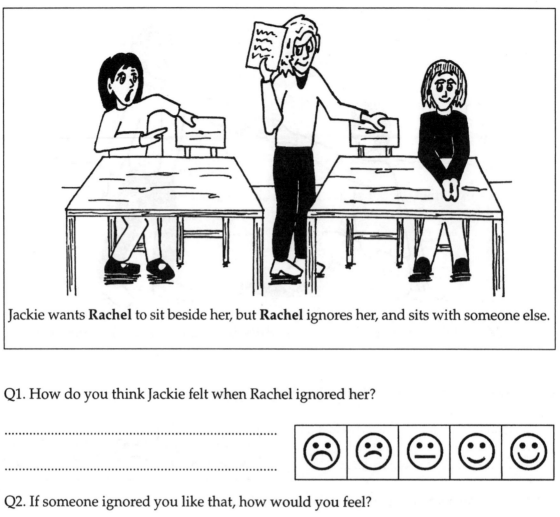

Jackie wants **Rachel** to sit beside her, but **Rachel** ignores her, and sits with someone else.

Q1. How do you think Jackie felt when Rachel ignored her?

....

....

Q2. If someone ignored you like that, how would you feel?

....

....

Q3. How do you think Rachel was feeling when she ignored Jackie?

....

....

Q4. If you ignored someone like that, how would you feel?

....

....

In the following activity, children are given the opportunity to develop their thinking about social behaviour by making comparative judgements about different behaviours. Children are asked to judge and compare different depicted behaviours on the basis of their relative acceptability or unacceptability. Forcing them to make such discriminations encourages children to think more carefully about the situations in question, and thereby enables them to develop their own understanding of interpersonal behaviour and of the rules governing such behaviour. In this activity, when comparing prosocial behaviours, children are asked to think about what is good about the depicted examples, which behaviours are relatively more acceptable or desirable, and why? When they are presented with examples of antisocial behaviour, the children are asked to think about what is bad about the depicted behaviours, which behaviours are relatively more unacceptable or undesirable, and why?

Activity 2 – Comparing social behaviours

Task adaptations for Activity 2

Rather than using all four examples of each category of behaviour as suggested for the 'good behaviour' and 'bad behaviour' ranking tasks described above, the tasks can be carried out on sub-sets of cartoons drawn from different categories. Thus, one example from each antisocial category could be selected to make a single comparison set (e.g. drawing numbers 46, 55, 61 and 72 – see Appendix).

For younger children, or where a simpler task would be more appropriate, teachers can reduce the number of behaviours to be compared within the comparison set. The simplest option, of course, would be to use pairs of cartoon behaviours in a paired comparison task. This would entail children answering a question such as, 'Which of these would please/upset you most?', and then being asked to explain their choice, as before. This can be repeated with as many pairs as considered appropriate. Interesting further possible variations of the paired comparison task are discussed in Chapter 7 where, for example, the comparison might be between boy characters and girl characters depicted in equivalent behaviour situations/episodes.

Activity 2	Comparing social behaviour
Purpose	To encourage children to make and to justify relative judgements about the 'goodness' of positive social behaviours; to encourage children to make and to justify relative judgements about the 'badness' of negative social behaviours.
Age/level	Age 10 and over.
Organisation	Individual or small-group activity.
Materials	(a) Four cartoon examples of each category of prosocial behaviour, and (b) four examples of each category of antisocial behaviour, each set presented on an A4 page as shown in Figure 6.3.
Instructions	(a) For each selected set of prosocial cartoons, e.g. the four examples of Lee being friendly (Figure 6.3), children first consider, "Which of these actions by Lee would please you the *most* if you were in the situation of the other child?" Then children identify the behaviour which they would see as "next best" and so on until they have put the four cartoon behaviours in rank order.
	(b) For each selected set of antisocial cartoons, e.g. the four examples of Ada being physically abusive (Figure 6.3), children first consider, "Which of these actions by Ada would upset you the *most* if you were in the situation of the other child – which is the worst behaviour?" Then children identify the behaviour which they would see as "next worst" and so on until they have put the four cartoon behaviours in rank order.
	Responses can be recorded on a simple task sheet (Figure 6.3) or may simply be given orally in an individual or small-group context.
Follow-up	Children can be asked to provide a few comments to explain the reasons for their rank ordering, either in written form as shown in Figure 6.3, or as part of a group discussion. Individual rankings can be collated as a small scale survey exercise followed by class discussion.

Figure 6.3 Comparing social behaviours (prosocial)

A

Lee and his friends are playing tig. Lee says to Peter, "Do you want to play?"

B

Lee sees a new boy at the school gate, and says, "Do you want to walk up the road with me?"

C

Simon is sitting alone in the dining hall. Lee asks, "Can I sit beside you?"

D

Lee asks Tim, "Do you want to come home to my house for tea?"

- Look at all four cartoon situations (A, B, C and D).
- Which of the four things that Lee did would you say was the nicest thing to do? In other words, if someone behaved like that to you, which would you find *most pleasing*?
- Fill in the 1st space below with your choice (A, B, C or D) and give your reason.
- Now put the other things Lee did in order, ending with the *least pleasing* thing he did in the 4th space, again giving reasons.

Choice	Cartoon	Reason for choice
1st (nicest, most pleasing)		
2nd		
3rd		
4th (least pleasing)		

Figure 6.3 (cont.) Comparing social behaviours (antisocial)

A
Gillian is walking in the school corridor, and **Ada** spits at her.

B
Ada sees Sandra across the street and throws a stone at her.

C
Ada doesn't like Penny, so she goes and kicks her.

D
Ada and her pals are bullying Anita after school.

- Look at all four cartoon situations (A, B, C and D).
- Which of the four things that Ada did would you say was the meanest thing to do? In other words, if someone behaved like that to you, which would you find *most upsetting*?
- Fill in the 1st space below with your choice (A, B, C or D), and give your reason.
- Now put the other things Ada did in order, ending with the *least upsetting* thing she did in the 4th space, again giving reasons.

Choice	Cartoon	Reason for choice
1st (most upsetting)		
2nd		
3rd		
4th (least upsetting)		

In this activity, children are given the opportunity to think about how they deal with different kinds of interpersonal behaviours they might encounter. It also encourages children to think about possible options, about different ways they might respond in a given situation. By requiring children to think about and explain the reasons for their responses to such behaviours, the activity engages them in examining their own values regarding interpersonal behaviour. Depending on the age of pupils, the task can be extended to involve children in moral questions of choices regarding social behaviour and underlying moral positions.

Experience of working with children on Activity 3 suggests that they tend to find it easier to say, and have *more* to say about how they would respond to antisocial behaviour than to prosocial behaviour. This bias is itself worth drawing children's attention to. Older primary and secondary pupils are capable of thinking about the question: 'Why should we find it easier to think of how to respond to 'bad' social behaviour than to 'good' social behaviour?' Experience also suggests that many children will say that if they do see misbehaviour, they would respond by reporting it to someone, usually their teacher. Again, this response highlights the bystander problem referred to earlier, and is worth exploring in class discussions about strategies for dealing with antisocial behaviours, such as bullying in school.

Activity 3 – Responding to good or bad behaviour

Activity 3	Responding to good or bad behaviour
Purposes	To encourage children to think about how they deal with interpersonal experiences; to enable children to develop their awareness of the range of possible ways to deal with different kinds of social interactions; to encourage children to evaluate their own responses to prosocial and antisocial behaviour.
Age/level	All ages.
Organisation	Individual activity followed by small group discussion. With younger pupils, teachers can sit with the group and work through the examples.
Materials	Teacher's selection from the stimulus set, response sheet (see Figure 6.4).
Instructions	For each cartoon, the child is asked the question, "If you were in this situation, and someone behaved like this towards you, what do you think you would do?" (With younger pupils, teacher guides children to focus on the victim of 'bad', or recipient of 'good' behaviour.) Then children should be asked to explain *why* they would respond in this way. In addition to the question of what the children **would** do, for older pupils, two further questions might be added: (1) "What else *could* you do in this situation?" which stimulates children to consider the range of options open to them; and (2) "What do you really think you *should* do in this situation?" which encourages children to make a moral decision and select the best strategy. Each of these further questions could also be followed by the question, "Why?" to encourage children to explain and justify their answers.
Follow-up	Group discussion focusing on comparisons of individual responses to the selected situations and reasons given for such responses is something all age groups can manage. Older children might be asked to look for patterns or categories in the individual responses, to compare 'typical' responses to different types of situation and possibly also to try to extract any general messages or implications from such patterns of responses (e.g. "Is there more we could do to encourage children to act kindly to one another in this school?").

Figure 6.4 Responding to good and bad behaviour

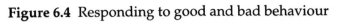

Michael kicks Jon and makes him drop his drink.

- If *you* were in this situation and someone like Michael did that to you, what would you do? (Write your answer in the space)

  ....

  Why? ....

- What other things *could* you do in a situation like this?

  ....

  ....

  ....

- Thinking about the situation again and all the things you could do, what do you think you really *should* do if you were in this situation? What would be the *best* thing for you to do?

  ....

  Why? ....

Activity 4 –
Discussion task:
exploring different
views

This activity is designed to encourage children to think about and justify their moral judgements about interpersonal behaviours in the context of group discussion/peer interaction. It has been shown that peer interaction is a potentially powerful strategy for teaching and learning in a wide range of curricular areas (Foot *et al.* 1990). In our research investigating the collaborative responses of groups of children to the cartoon behaviours, we found that the most productive discussions were generated by single-sex groups of three children. In mixed sex groupings there was a tendency for the majority, be it of boys or girls, to dominate the discussion and decision making. In the classroom context, teachers may nevertheless prefer mixed sex groupings and may need to use larger groups to fit local circumstances.

Task adaptations for Activity 4

With younger children, or those who may be less confident in their oral discussion skills, the group task can be simplified from ranking four examples to choosing the one example which is the worst or most unpleasant (in the case of antisocial examples), or best or most desirable (in the case of prosocial examples). Depending on the children's capacity for meaningful comparisons, it may be more appropriate for groups to work with fewer than four cartoons in the comparison set. For example, pairs of cartoons could be selected for simpler, direct paired comparison.

Extending the core
activities in the
school context

The activities described in this chapter were designed to encourage children to think about and develop their own understanding of interpersonal behaviour. Wherever possible teachers should look for the opportunity to challenge children in this aspect of their learning. One of the best ways of doing this is to ask children to make connections between issues arising out of planned curricular activities of the kind discussed in this chapter and the real context for their social behaviour, namely the school community. For example, Activity 3 leads naturally into discussion of school rules and strategies. The following chapter considers in some detail further extensions and variations on the 'themes' established in the core activities presented above.

Activity 4	**Exploring different views of social behaviour**
Purposes	To encourage children to express, and share with others, their judgements about social behaviour; to enhance children's understanding of social behaviour through collaborative decision making; to encourage children to explain and justify their judgements about prosocial and antisocial behaviour, and to evaluate the judgements of others; to provide children with a context in which to apply their moral reasoning concerning social behaviour.
Age/level	10 years and over.
Organisation	Small group task. Groups of three work best, but groups of four and five are also effective.
Materials	Sets of four cartoons representing each of the eight categories of behaviour.
Instructions	Construct various sets of four prosocial (or four antisocial) behaviours, by selecting *one* example from each prosocial (or antisocial) category set. Thus, for example, a prosocial set will include an example of *caring*, *sharing*, *helping* and *inclusion*. Children should be asked to put the four behaviours in order, starting with the 'best' (prosocial behaviours), or the 'worst' (antisocial behaviours). Children should first make an individual, independent response, using the activity sheet suggested for Activity 2 (Figure 6.3). Then working together as a group, children should be asked to share their individual rank orderings of the four cartoon behaviours in each set, to discuss their reasons for the relative judgements made and to work towards producing an agreed group rank order for each set of four cartoons.
Follow-up	A valuable follow-up activity would be to encourage the children to reflect on the kinds of reasons they had given for their selections of best and/or worst social behaviours. A worthwhile focus is for each different working group to present and justify its decisions to the rest of the class. Older children can be encouraged to be constructively critical about the level of argument of the group. Group discussion focusing on the process of group decision making is very worthwhile, if time allows. Children can be asked to consider what made it difficult or easy to arrive at a group decision.

Chapter 7

Variations on a Theme

The basic tasks we have described in Chapter 6 afford children the opportunity to attend to the emotional components of interpersonal behaviours (Activity 1); to make and to justify their relative judgements about different pro- and anti-social behaviours (Activity 2); to consider different ways of responding to other children's social behaviours (Activity 3); and to develop skills of interpersonal communication, evaluation and explanation in relation to such behaviours (Activity 4). However, in introducing these activities in the classroom or at home, teachers and parents will readily perceive that the materials may be used in a variety of ways. In this chapter, we make some suggestions for other tasks which can be both interesting for children, and beneficial for their interpersonal thinking and social behaviour, but readers should feel in no way constrained by our proposals. The central aims of focusing children's attention upon, and assisting their awareness of interpersonal behaviours may be achieved by other, more innovative or locally relevant uses of these or similar materials.

The activities described below are designed to focus more directly on the *personal experiences* of individual children (Activity 5), to make children think about *both the intentions and the consequences* of social behaviours (Activity 6), to consider *gender differences* in attitudes towards social behaviours (Activity 7), and to afford children an opportunity for *role playing*, both as a device for raising their awareness of intentions and consequences of social behaviours, and to provide practice in ways of responding to antisocial behaviours (Activity 8).

Activity 5 – Children's personal experiences of social interactions

While the social behaviours depicted in the cartoon drawings are all based upon examples from children's own experiences, individual children clearly have their own stories to tell, and personal experiences can provide material for more meaningful and educationally profitable classroom discussions. Of course, there will be sensitive incidents of, particularly, antisocial behaviours which children may be reluctant to divulge openly, and teachers must judge when class discussions or individual activities are more appropriate. In a supportive context, children's individual experiences of peer social behaviours can be used as a basis for peer group and class discussion about motives, consequences and appropriate response strategies in interpersonal behaviours.

Activity 5	**Personal experiences of pro- and anti-social behaviours**
Purposes	Finding ways to elicit individual children's experience, as actor or recipient, of pro- and anti-social peer behaviour, and to use such examples as a basis for discussion and group activity.
Organisation	Individual, pairs and small group activities. Children should be encouraged to select peers in the paired and group activities.
Materials	Paper and pencils.
Methods	*(a) Individual tasks* Ask child to narrate, write down, or draw an example of prosocial or antisocial behaviour that they have experienced personally, namely "Tell me (draw me a picture) about a time when another child did some-thing to you that was nice (nasty), that made you feel happy (upset)." *(b) Working in pairs* In a form of role play, ask children to interview each other, e.g. as if for a local newspaper or TV news report, or as a witness in court. Using the same instructions as in (a) above, the child interviewer seeks a report on the interviewee's own experience of pro- or anti-social peer behaviour, which can be written down, drawn or even tape-recorded. *(c) Discussion and support groups.* With children's consent, their examples can be used as a basis for peer discussion: pairs or groups of children should work to agree answers to the following questions: Why did this behaviour happen? What is the best response? (How) should this behaviour be encouraged or discouraged? Such questions can also be addressed in class discussion with the teacher.
Follow-up	Class discussion of the answers achieved in paired and group sessions can lead to the development of class rules on interpersonal behaviours, both supporting prosocial and discouraging antisocial, which are driven by the children's own experiences and suggestions.
Age levels	All age levels. The manner of elicitation in individual tasks will depend upon the oral, writing and drawing skills of children, as well as their willingness to share their experiences. Likewise, children's level of autonomy will dictate the degree of supervision necessary in paired and group work.

Activity 6 – Thinking about intentions and consequences

Young children's natural tendency in social interactions is to view the event in terms of its effect upon themselves first; thinking about the effect an interaction might have on other participants is secondary; giving consideration to the reasons for someone's behaviour, to their motives for behaving in this or that way, is for them an even less salient perspective. However, it is just these latter considerations, being aware of the effect one's behaviour has on others, and of the intentions of one's partner in an interaction, that form the basis of prosocial behaviour. The following task is therefore designed to focus children's attention upon *intentions* and *consequences* in social interactions. Children are invited to speculate about the precipitating factors which led to a given interaction, and the ensuing consequences of that interaction, both in terms of the behaviours of the participants, and their thoughts and feelings at the time. This task can be particularly effective if groups of children discuss social behaviours experienced by the individual members, such that they are trying to work out what one of their group did actually do, think and feel in a real situation. Where appropriate, it can also be useful to place bullies and victims in the same groups, such that they are encouraged to share different perspectives.

Activity 7 – Exploring sex differences

An intriguing aspect of children's socialisation has always been the differences which become apparent between boys and girls, in their communication style, their social attitudes and behaviour. While both sexes are equally capable of behaving well and behaving badly, they typically choose different ways and different occasions to do so. Although such differences may have a genetic component, we can certainly assume that the learning of gender stereotypes has a powerful influence. Recent researchers (e.g. Gilligan 1982) have proposed that, while male attitudes to socio-moral behaviour are dominated by rules, and considerations of fairness and justice, females are more concerned with the ethics of care and emotional support. That being the case, it will be instructive for boys and girls to openly consider and debate their differing viewpoints on particular pro- and anti-social peer interactions. Is a particular behaviour perceived more positively by boys than by girls? Is it more acceptable when performed by a girl than by a boy? Do girls and boys have different views on the prosocial behaviours that are important, or the antisocial behaviours that are unacceptable? In exploring these questions, the limited set of mixed sex cartoons, depicting one example of each of the four prosocial and four antisocial behaviours, can be used in combination with their matched same sex drawings. Thus, for example, representing the prosocial behaviour of *helping*, we have mixed sex versions in which Katie helps Billy (cartoon 38), and Billy helps Katie (37); and corresponding same sex versions in which Billy helps Todd (20), and Katie helps Emma (24). What differences do children perceive between Katie helping Billy or Emma, and between Billy helping Katie and helping Todd?

Activity 6	Thinking about intentions and consequences
Purposes	To help children to think about the causes and consequences of social behaviours, namely about (a) what might have prompted a particular behaviour, and what the participants in the interaction were thinking and/or feeling before it occurred, and (b) what might happen, and what the participants are thinking and feeling, as a result of the interaction.
Organisation	Individual, paired, small group or class activities.
Materials	Any combination of up to six different social behaviours, taken from the cartoon set, or from children's own experiences – see Activity 5. For the thinking and feeling questions, described below, thought bubbles could be added to the drawings, above the relevant characters.
Methods	Present the drawings one at a time, and focus on *one* of the characters, either the actor or the receiver. The aim is for children, individually or in pairs/groups, to tell, or write a story from the viewpoint of that character, in answer to at least some of the prompt questions shown: *(a) Focusing on the actor* (see Figure 7.1) What was X (the actor) doing just before s/he did/said that to Y? How do you think s/he was feeling before s/he did it? What was s/he thinking about, and why did s/he do it? Now that s/he has done it, how do you think s/he'll be feeling? Have you ever done this? How did you feel? *(b) Focusing on the receiver* (see Figure 7.2) What was Y (the receiver) doing just before X did that? How do you think Y was feeling before it happened? What was s/he thinking about? What will Y do now? How do you think s/he'll be feeling? What will Y be thinking about? Has this ever happened to you? How did you feel?
Follow-up	Each child's or group's story can be presented to the class, either written, narrated, or perhaps acted out (see Activity 8), and class discussion can focus on different interpretations of the characters' thoughts, feelings and behaviours.
Age levels	Given the imaginative nature of this task, it may prove too difficult for children younger than 8 years; for 8–10 year-olds too, some reduction will probably be necessary in the number of questions asked.

Figure 7.1 Thinking about the actor

Lee and his friends are playing tig. **Lee** says to Peter, "Do you want to play?" | **Jane** and her friends are gossiping and saying nasty things about Helen.

Q1. Before he saw Peter standing there, what was Lee doing?

Q2. When he saw Peter, what do you think Lee was thinking or feeling?

Q3. Why did Lee ask Peter to play?

Q4. How would you describe Lee?

Q5. If Peter wants (doesn't want) to play, how will Lee feel?

Q6. Have you ever done what Lee did? How did you feel?

Q1. Before she saw Helen, what do you think Jane was doing?

Q2. When she saw Helen coming, what was Jane thinking or feeling?

Q3. Why do you think Jane is gossiping about Helen?

Q4. Do you think Jane is enjoying herself? Why?

Q5. What does Jane really think about Helen?

Q6. Have you ever gossiped and said nasty things about someone? How did you feel?

Figure 7.2 Thinking about the receiver

Nicola is stuck with her classwork. **Katie** tries to help her. | **Dan** grabs Alec's bag and throws it over the school fence.

Q1. Before Katie helped her, what was Nicola thinking about?

Q2. How was she feeling about her work?

Q3. What does Nicola think about Katie helping her?

Q4. How would you describe Nicola?

Q5. Have you ever been stuck like Nicola? How did you feel?

Q1. What was Alec doing before Dan came along?

Q2. How did he feel when he saw Dan coming?

Q3. When Dan grabbed his bag, what did he think?

Q4. What did he feel when the bag went over the fence?

Q5. What will Alec do now?

Q6. Has anything like that ever happened to you? How did you feel?

Note In the above examples, the aim is to get children thinking about the thoughts, feelings, intentions and reactions of a child behaving prosocially or antisocially. The prompt questions shown are suggestions which can be varied as appropriate to each drawing.

Activity 7 Exploring sex differences

Purposes   To encourage girls and boys to share and compare their views about behaving well and behaving badly. What expectations do they have of each other? What behaviours matter to them, and why?

Organisation   Individual tasks, same sex and mixed sex pairs or small groups.

Materials   Combinations of same sex and mixed sex drawings of different behaviours, selected from the set.

Methods   *(a) Ranking same-sex drawings* (see Figure 7.3)

Begin by creating matched sets of boys' and girls' prosocial and antisocial behaviours. For example, from the set of girls' drawings, select one example of each of the four prosocial behaviours, and then select the equivalent drawings from the boys' set (see Figure 7.3). In this way, various matched sets of prosocial behaviours, and of antisocial behaviours can be created, as required.

In groups, set children the task of ranking one such set of either prosocial or antisocial behaviours (use Response Sheet for Activity 2 (Figure 6.3)), such that some groups are ranking girls' behaviours, and other groups are ranking equivalent boys' behaviours. The children's task is to achieve consensus within their groups. Each group's agreed ranking can then be written on the blackboard, or on an OHP, and group members asked to explain and justify their ranking to the class. The class teacher can focus discussion on reasons for differences in the rankings of equivalent boys' and girls' behaviours.

A further dimension can be added to this task by employing same sex groups of children, to see whether the two sexes differentially rank boy and girl behaviours.

(b) Comparing same-sex and mixed-sex interactions (see Figure 7.4)

The mixed sex set of drawings depicts two versions of a selected sub-set of behaviours, one from each of the behaviour categories, namely a male actor and female recipient (M-F) and a female actor and male recipient (F-M). For each depicted behaviour, select the same sex (M-M and F-F) drawings which match the mixed sex versions (see Figure 7.4). Individuals or same sex groups can make the following comparisons:

Focus on recipient: Present girls with F-F and M-F versions (Figure 7.4, C and A) and boys with M-M and F-M versions (Figure 7.4, B and D). Ask children to identify with the recipient, and to say which interaction they would prefer to happen to them (prosocial), or which would most upset them (antisocial), and to discuss why.

Focus on the actor: Present girls with the F-F and the F-M versions (Figure 7.4, C and D), and boys with the M-M and M-F versions (Figure 7.4, B and A). Ask children to identify with the actor, and for each comparison, to imagine which situation would most please (prosocial), or upset (antisocial) their friends (or their mother, or their teacher), and to discuss why.

Outcomes   Both group and class results of the above tasks can be collated, by the groups themselves, or as a teacher-led class activity, and can form the basis of reports for the school magazines, or home-based research, or further classwork on sex differences, sex discrimination, or values education.

Age levels   10 years upwards.

Figure 7.3 Ranking boys' and girls' behaviours

Note Any combination of matched prosocial or antisocial behaviours can be used in this task. Set some groups the task of ranking boys' behaviours, while other groups rank girls' behaviours. Alternatively, simply ask groups to decide on the best (prosocial) or worst (antisocial) behaviour in their set, and to explain why. Compare choices and explanations for boys' and girls' behaviours.

Figure 7.4 Comparing same-sex and mixed-sex interactions

The examples below show four versions of a prosocial behaviour, one child sharing lunch with another: a boy sharing with a girl (A), and with another boy (B), and a girl sharing with another girl (C), and with a boy (D). There are eight such sets of four versions of the same behaviour, as follows:

Caring: Cartoons 2, 6, 33, 34.   *Sharing*: Cartoons 9, 13, 35, 36.   *Helping*: Cartoons 20, 24, 37, 38.
Inclusion: 27, 31, 39, 40.   *Verbal abuse*: 41, 45, 73, 74.   *Physical abuse*: 49, 53, 75, 76.
Rejection: 59, 63, 77, 78.   *Delinquency*: 65, 69, 79, 80.

A. Alison has forgotten her lunch, so **Peter** is sharing his lunch with her.

B. Jim has forgotten his lunch, so **Peter** is sharing his with him.

C. June has forgotten her lunch, so **Alison** is sharing hers with June.

D. Peter has forgotten his lunch, so **Alison** is sharing her lunch with him.

This task has two parts. In the first part, children identify with the recipient of a behaviour, prosocial or antisocial, and consider how they would feel if it was a boy or a girl who behaved like that to them. In the second part, they identify with the actor, and consider how they would feel behaving like that to a boy or to a girl.

Part 1. In the first part of this task, focusing on the recipient, cartoons A and C would be shown to girls, and cartoons B and D would be shown to boys. The children should be asked to identify with the recipient, and to respond to such questions as –
Q1. Which is more likely, that a boy or a girl would do that to you?
Q2. Which would you most like to happen to you? Why? (or most dislike, for an antisocial behaviour)
Q3. Would you feel differently if it was a boy like Peter, or a girl like Alison who was sharing with you? In what way?

Note: In order to assist children to identify with the character and to make comparisons, the character names should be changed where necessary to make them the same. Thus, in the above example, when presenting cartoons A and C to girls, the recipient's name should be June in both cases, i.e. Alison shares with June (C), and Peter shares with June (A).
Exactly the same procedure should be followed with antisocial behaviours, encouraging children to identify with the same sex victim of the behaviour, and compare their responses when the actor is male or female.

Part 2. The other part of this task requires children to focus on the actor in each interaction, and to make the relevant comparisons, namely in the above example, Alison shares her lunch with June (C) and with Peter (D). Ask girls to identify with Alison, and respond to such questions as –
Q1. Is it more likely that you would do that to a boy or a girl? Why?
Q2. Do you think it is nicer to do it to a boy or a girl? Which would your friends/teacher/mother think or say?
Q3. Would you feel differently doing it to a boy or a girl? How would you feel?

Activity 8 – Role-playing prosocial and antisocial behaviours

Role-playing is already used as an educational strategy when promoting aspects of children's behavioural learning. For example, many safety training programmes, such as the Kidscape programme, which aim to improve children's ability to protect themselves from potential abuse, both physical and sexual, use role-play exercises as a means of developing appropriate behavioural skills. In the present context, our primary intention is to develop children's sensitivity to the interpersonal feelings of children involved in social interactions, and to the motives and consequences of their behaviours. By enacting various pro- and anti-social peer interactions, and alternating their roles as actor and as recipient, children can learn to adopt different perspectives on social behaviour, to consider how it feels to be both the donor and the recipient of such behaviours, to rehearse and discuss the responses best suited to the circumstances, and the consequences of such responses. In approaching this task, we suggest that the class should focus upon one social behaviour at a time, e.g. verbal abuse, and use one pictorial example of this behaviour as a basis for forming a storyline. A brief script can be developed, filling in such details as what preceded the interaction in the drawing, the personality of the characters and their familiarity with each other, the motives of the actor, and a possible response for the victim. The essence of this technique lies in the involvement of children at three stages – firstly in developing the script, then in role-playing the interaction, and finally in exploring the feelings and responses of the characters both during and consequent upon the interaction. The first and third stages can initially be achieved best as teacher-led class activities, although with a little experience children can work in small groups, with each group having an opportunity to role-play their own script.

The activities described in this and the previous chapter by no means exhaust the possibilities for teachers who wish to encourage children's thinking about interpersonal behaviours. They are suggestions only, and will, we hope, provide the basis for many other activities which teachers and children can develop together. Within the classroom, many more locally relevant examples of children's social interactions can be discussed and used as task material. The important thing is that children come to perceive social behaviour as an enjoyable and beneficial educational topic to which they themselves have much to contribute. Values education and children's personal and social development constitute part of the school's remit, in preparing children for life in the community, and it is to this broader context of the relationship between school and community that we now turn in our concluding chapter.

Activity 8	**Role playing social interactions**
Purposes	To develop children's sensitivity to the causes and consequences of their social behaviours, and to rehearse appropriate response strategies.
Organisation	Teacher-led class activity and small group tasks.
Materials	Individual drawings, selected from set as appropriate to the lesson focus, and displayed on OHP if possible.
Methods	*(a) Developing a script* Scripts should be devised to include such details as: the location of the interaction (playground, street, etc.), the presence of onlookers (adults or other children, etc.), what the participants were doing before the interaction, a brief dialogue between the characters before, during and after the interaction itself, and the participants' actions after the event. Scripts should first be based upon a cartoon drawing selected from the set, and can be devised as a teacher-led whole class activity. With experience, however, script preparation can become a small group activity, possibly based upon the children's own experiences, with only limited guidance from the teacher as required. *(b) Role playing the interaction* Casting the players, main and supporting, can initially be voluntary, but children's enthusiasm for role play will increase when they create their own scripts in small groups, and over a period of time all children should have a chance to role-play one of the interactions. Each interaction should be played twice, with the same children switching characters (e.g. bully–victim). *(c) Discussing the role play* Each role-play should be the focus for a discussion, either whole class or small group, of reasons, feelings and responses concomitant with the interaction. Why did the actor behave like that? How did each character feel during the interaction? How should the recipient respond? What is the best response? Could or should others (adults or children) become involved? The thoughts and feelings of the role-playing children are particularly relevant here.
Age levels	Simplified versions of role plays can be successful from 7–8 years upwards, but script development and post-performance discussion gain in complexity and value from 10–11 years upwards.

Chapter 8

Practical Contexts for Prosocial Behaviour

Personal and social development involves a wide range of teaching strategies. Within these there will be particular emphasis on active or experiential learning, the basis for which could be either authentic experiences of pupils which happen in the home, the school or the community or experiences created by the teacher for a specific purpose. (SOED 1993, p. 3)

Learning through experience is an important and effective way of making learning real and meaningful for all young people. By building and sustaining genuine and empathetic relationships with and amongst their pupils, teachers can enhance an aspect of learning that is always authentically experiential. Such interdependent and evolving relationships are central to effective education for personal and social growth. (SCCC 1995, p. 12)

The inclusive school

As we discussed in Chapter 2, the school itself, by virtue of the ethos it promotes, can provide the context for teaching social behaviour and fostering children's personal and social development. This chapter looks at some specific initiatives and strategies designed to create practical contexts in which to foster prosocial behaviour through active, experiential learning, not only in school but also in the wider community. The concept of the 'inclusive' school (SCCC 1995) can be taken as a guiding principle for such initiatives. According to the definition cited in Chapter 2, the inclusive school is one in which *all* feel they are respected, valued and cared for, and in which the perspectives of parents, the wider community and the young people themselves are taken into account. How can children be encouraged to develop this sense of belonging to their school, of being cared for and included, through which they can develop as responsible individuals with an appreciation of the value of positive relationships and a commitment to prosocial behaviour?

Clearly, one essential attribute of the inclusive school is that it must be a 'listening' school. That children must be given the opportunity to express their views on all matters affecting them is a fundamental principle of the United Nations Convention on the Rights of the Child, now enshrined in UK legislation in the 1989 Children Act and the 1995 Children (Scotland) Act. Therefore, schools no longer have any real option: they are obliged by legislation to listen to children. Regrettably, some have reacted with hostility to the challenge of opening up procedures and decision making within schools, arguing on the grounds that children need first to become capable of exercising responsibility and that children (especially young children) are simply not competent genuinely to participate in decision making. However, these and other hostile arguments can be readily refuted (see Lansdown 1996). Children must be shown respect in order to learn to be respectful of others and one of the most direct and significant ways in which respect can be shown to a child is to listen to, and take seriously, what the child has to say. Let us consider some specific ways in which this can be achieved.

The listening school

Circle time

Circle time is a well established routine in many classrooms, encompassing a wide range of activities in the domain of education for PSD (see, for example, Mosely 1996). Its hallmarks are acceptance, inclusion, respect and sharing: in other words, activities which are consistent with prosocial values. Circle time is a time to come together as a class and share thoughts, experiences and feelings in a very supportive context. Rules of engagement should be simple and clear. Firstly the circle time must be given a regular and significant 'slot' in the timetabled curriculum (many teachers choose to start, or end, each day with circle time), and it should be protected against the predations of other, potentially expansive elements of the curriculum. Beyond that, White (1990) suggests just three simple rules: only one person should speak at a time, everyone can have fun, and no one can spoil anyone else's fun. By providing the consistent, secure framework of the circle time routine, teachers can give children the confidence to express their feelings openly, including their feelings about themselves and about each other. It is important that everyone has the opportunity to speak, but that no one is obliged to do so. Typically, circle time involves some kind of 'round' where the teacher might provide a sentence or phrase which each child is invited to complete, such as, 'What makes me really happy is. . .'. Handled well, circle time can be not only a way to boost children's self-esteem, but also a means by which to facilitate their exploration of ideas and their reflection on emotional and social experiences in such a way as to promote moral understanding. It is particularly helpful in this context to encourage children to formulate and share their questions about the issues being discussed and for the teacher to ensure that children's questions are valued and given serious consideration. 'At its best, circle time . . . allows pupils to make meaning of inner and outer worlds.' (Housego and Burns 1994, p. 25.)

However, if handled less thoughtfully, circle time can be superficial and of very limited value. In such situations, when their 'turn' comes, children may simply comply with the surface characteristics of the activity by making brief, discrete statements, without engaging in worthwhile thinking or attempting to relate to, or build on, previous contributions. As Housego and Burns (1994) point out in their critique of circle time, there is an inherent danger in one of the core features of circle time, namely, the acceptance of all children's contributions, which is that the teacher may feel disinclined to offer comment, to challenge or question what children have to say. Thus the opportunity for children to learn and to extend their understanding is lost.

Circle time can provide a vehicle for the kinds of group discussions which were described in Chapters 6 and 7, as follow-up activities. It can also be an appropriate strategy for the initial orientation of pupils to working with the materials. A single cartoon selected from the set could, for example, be the stimulus to which each child in turn makes a personal response by trying to empathise with the depicted characters.

Pupil Councils

In order to ensure that children have their views heard, many schools have successfully introduced Pupil Councils, or pupil representation on school councils, providing a forum for the expression of children's opinions about matters affecting the whole school community. The ultimate expression of this procedure was provided by A. S. Neill's Summerhill School, in which all pupils and staff met in regular whole school meetings to debate matters of policy and democratically to decide on, and administer, school rules. Many schools are now involved in similar, if less inclusive, initiatives which are seen as being consistent with the idea of 'citizenship education'. What is essential here is that the forum or council is not merely a 'talking shop', but rather that it has a real purpose and genuine capability to make things happen in the school community. Where this is the case, such as in Allan's Primary School in Stirling, which was recently reported as having successfully introduced a Pupil Council, schools have been pleased with the benefits shown in improved pupil learning and enhanced school ethos (Ross 1996). The Pupil Council itself might comprise only a relatively small number of pupils, typically two or three from each year group, but its potential value extends far beyond that number. In each class the procedures of the whole-school Pupil Council can be mirrored in class discussions with a view to identifying concerns which can be taken by the pupil representative to the full council for consideration. Thus, the voices of all pupils can be heard in true democratic fashion. Indeed, emulating the functions of local democracy within the classroom can be a very powerful way of helping children learn about this aspect of citizenship. Most importantly, an effective Pupil Council is a way to foster positive social values and to encourage socially responsible behaviour within the school and potentially in the wider community. Having a broader outlook on the role of the school in its community is another important attribute of the inclusive, caring school, which provides the optimum context for personal and social development.

In an inclusive, caring school, every opportunity should be taken to encourage children not only to behave in a socially responsible way but also to reflect on their behaviour. One example of an initiative of this kind would be the introduction of a *buddy system*, whereby older pupils, especially, but not exclusively, in secondary schools, look out for the welfare of younger pupils. Over a period of time, as the 'buddy' relationship grows stronger, pupils can gain confidence to deal themselves with problems that might arise for them in school. Furthermore, there are personal and social gains in this kind of scheme both for the children who receive support and for the children who act as the buddy. Another similar idea has been tried successfully in secondary schools, particularly where there has been concern about bullying, namely, *peer counselling*. In this kind of scheme, older children are organised to provide a 'listening ear' to children who might be experiencing problems of victimisation. An example of such an initiative is the 'Friends against Bullying' (FAB) system developed at Hermitage Academy in Helensburgh (Mair and MacDonald 1993). A frequent finding in the survey research into bullying is the low rate of reporting to teachers (less than 50%, according to Whitney and Smith 1993). Experience suggests that children may feel more inclined to disclose such information to another child than to a teacher. For peer counselling to be successful, the counsellors must be provided with careful guidance and training. The same is true of the third example of a scheme to encourage caring and helping among children in school, *peer tutoring*. In this case, the focus of the helping relationship is on learning in key areas of the curriculum, such as language, mathematics and science, but the gains for both tutor and tutee are not confined to academic, cognitive areas of learning; rather it would appear that being involved in peer tutoring again confers potential personal and social benefits to all concerned (Foot *et al.* 1990; Topping 1988).

If the school is to be a caring community, its policies should reflect the ideas and expressed wishes of the children by fully involving pupils in whole-school policy making. As part of the remit of a Pupil Council, children might be asked to shape school policy by devising a code of playground behaviour, emphasising positive, friendly behaviour. Though it can prove a difficult thing to do, as rules have a tendency to emerge as a series of 'do not' prohibitions, children should nevertheless be asked to try to frame such rules positively.

The school as a caring community

Responsibility for the school environment

In addition to making suggestions about the rules of playground behaviour, children can be involved in practical aspects of planning improvements in the playground itself. This can grow into a very substantial project with potential links across all areas of the curriculum. Where such work is done in a genuinely collaborative manner it can meet many of the requirements for effective education for PSD. Pupils can take responsibility for listening to, and carefully collating, the views of children and other members of the school community. By organising a proper forum for such collated views to be aired and debated, children can be given the opportunity to make and justify decisions, after having first acknowledged and attempted to reconcile different viewpoints. Engaging children in projects of this kind potentially develops another strand of the curriculum for PSD, as conceptualised by SOED (1993), namely, *independence and inter-dependence*. In presenting children with the challenge of taking responsibility to solve meaningful, practical problems in their own environment, schools can foster creativity, innovation and collaboration, which are seen by SOED (1993) as vital elements in the development of independence and interdependence. Furthermore, through this kind of activity, children's awareness of the complexity of the social context in which they live can be developed, along with their awareness of the need for flexibility in their own personal responses to the social challenges they face. Where the problem solving activity is genuinely collaborative, children will have the opportunity to develop their interpersonal skills as well as an understanding of interdependence. The caring approach we have referred to throughout this chapter and this awareness of interdependence can, of course, be progressively extended beyond the school and its community to encompass issues of more global significance.

Confronting antisocial behaviour

While the emphasis here has been on the caring school and on prosocial values, there will always remain a need to equip children to address and confront antisocial behaviour, and a concomitant need for schools to work to identify and try to counter unfairness and discrimination in all its manifestations. In the case of bullying, the work of Alan Mclean (1994) has highlighted the importance of the issue of 'bystander apathy', which we touched on in Chapter 2. Bullying is most often a behaviour to which there are many child witnesses; such bystanders need to be encouraged to act in defence of the victim more often than appears spontaneously to be the case. Racial and sexual harassment remain widespread in society and also in schools. Schools should work to achieve an ethos in which such behaviours are clearly understood to be unacceptable, and perpetrators should expect the opprobrium of all their peers who witness such acts. To bring about such an ethos will involve a long term commitment to shift the prevalent culture in schools, and will require the collaboration of all concerned, including parents, for it to be fully effective.

The focus of this chapter has been on prosocial behaviour and how it can be promoted. Prosocial behaviour will be nurtured where, as far as possible, positive social values are shared by all concerned. That these values can find expression in socially responsible behaviour is evident in recent initiatives in the area of citizenship education. In a number of such projects children have been encouraged to behave prosocially towards other children in their class and in their school as a whole. In others, the prosocial behaviour has been directed purposefully towards members of the wider community through a range of school–community projects. In Golspie High School, for example, secondary pupils work for 'Young Volunteers in Action Citizenship Awards' under a scheme organised by the Scottish Community Education Council and linked to existing modules in PSE. One of their projects entailed children raising the funds to build a greenhouse for residents of an old people's home; thereafter, the pupils continued to help with gardening on a regular basis, building and maintaining a relationship with the old people in the home (Tahir 1996). The value of such a project for the children involved extends into many different areas of their learning and their development as individuals and as citizens. Increased self-awareness and interpersonal skills were among the expected outcomes, together with organisational ability and various practical skills associated with the kind of work involved. Therefore, such initiatives not only provide a clear focus for prosocial behaviour, but may also be claimed to contribute significantly to the education of the 'whole child'.

We would suggest that schools contemplating such an initiative should bear the following guidelines in mind:

- encourage children before they embark on planning any project to assess carefully its likely value to the community group concerned;
- encourage children to build on and extend existing links with other agencies, professionals and members of the community (e.g. other local schools and pre-5 establishments, community police, community education service, health services and caring agencies);
- let pupils themselves take as much responsibility as possible for determining the direction of the project and for managing it (e.g. through the Pupil Council, if such exists, or some other representative group);
- encourage children to identify their own and each other's strengths which can be brought to bear on the project;
- provide opportunities for informal self- and peer-assessment as part of the monitoring of the success of the project (e.g. through pupils being requested to provide regular progress reports to the teacher, or head teacher, and the rest of the school).

Citizenship education and community action

Community Action Projects

In the secondary school, such voluntary community projects might be organised to some extent at least by small groups of pupils themselves, in consultation with teachers, other relevant professionals, community agencies and, of course, members of the community. In primary and special schools, clearly there is more need for the teacher to be involved in the planning of the project. A strong case can be made for community action to provide the focus for teachers' planning of project work or class topics in the primary school and special school, with benefits to pupil learning extending across all curricular areas in addition to PSD.

The Community Action Project is an ideal vehicle for the promotion of prosocial values, and for fostering the prosocial behaviours discussed in previous chapters, namely, *helping, sharing, caring* and *including*, in a real context with a genuine purpose. Such a project should be planned just as thoroughly as any other 'curricular' topic or study, ideally in close consultation with community and other agencies. In parallel with the above-mentioned example of the secondary school project based in an old people's home, there are many successful examples of projects involving a partnership between primary schools and agencies working for the elderly. Groups of children can be given the opportunity to befriend and visit on a regular basis elderly people living in the community, for example, in a neighbouring nursing home. There have been several such projects where one of the purposes was for the children to carry out research in local oral history. Such initiatives clearly encourage children to respect and value what the elderly person has to say, and to show this respect by asking appropriate questions and genuinely listening to the answers. The children must also learn important social skills in order to negotiate and maintain the contact required in such a project, which can culminate in the children providing a report of their findings to the senior citizens involved. Expressive Arts may also provide an appropriate focus for the children's learning in a Community Action Project in which case the children can feel that they are contributing to the wellbeing of the elderly people by their performances in the visual arts, music or drama. Local initiatives of this kind involving partnerships between teachers and other professionals, such as community artists, working either in the school or in the wider community can be particularly effective (Riccio and Gordon 1996).

In Scotland, the Community Education Service has been the 'umbrella' under which community action projects might take place and interprofessional partnership between school and community education staff has proved fruitful in identifying and targeting community needs to make such projects worthwhile. It is important to distinguish between the kind of direct action in the community being advocated here and conventional charitable fund-raising activity, where the efforts of the children are only indirectly prosocial. While, of course, there will always be a place for fund-raising activities in schools, it is preferable to engage children, where possible, directly in helping, sharing with, and caring for real people. There is a genuine challenge here for schools to make service in the community a dynamic, enjoyable and worthwhile experience for children, but one which is undoubtedly worth the effort of all concerned to ensure children gain first hand experiences of genuine prosocial behaviour.

Conclusion

In this book we have argued that children's social behaviour is something which should be given more serious consideration as part of the school curriculum. There is much to be learned by all parties about the perceptions and understandings of children in this domain of their experience, particularly in the complex area of interpersonal relationships. We are confident that, by engaging children in thinking about and discussing the whole spectrum of social behaviour we will help them to develop their social understanding. Education for personal and social growth will be particularly effective where, in addition to the focused classroom activities presented here, teachers engage children practically in contexts designed to elicit prosocial behaviour, both within the school and in the wider community. However, what is perhaps most important of all, in the words of SCCC (1995) quoted at the beginning of this chapter, is the need for teachers to strive to build and sustain *genuine and empathetic relationships with and amongst their pupils'*.

List of Cartoon Drawings

Same sex

Cartoons 1–4	Boys caring	
Cartoons 5–8	Girls caring	
Cartoons 9–12	Boys sharing	
Cartoons 13–16	Girls sharing	
Cartoons 17–20	Boys helping	
Cartoons 21–24	Girls helping	
Cartoons 25–28	Boys including	
Cartoons 29–32	Girls including	

Mixed sex

Cartoons 33–34	Caring
Cartoons 35–36	Sharing
Cartoons 37–38	Helping
Cartoons 39–40	Including

Prosocial behaviours

Same sex

Cartoons 41–44	Boys – verbal abuse
Cartoons 45–48	Girls – verbal abuse
Cartoons 49–52	Boys – physical abuse
Cartoons 53–56	Girls – physical abuse
Cartoons 57–60	Boys – rejection
Cartoons 61–64	Girls – rejection
Cartoons 65–68	Boys – delinquency
Cartoons 69–72	Girls – delinquency

Mixed sex

Cartoons 73–74	Verbal abuse
Cartoons 75–76	Physical abuse
Cartoons 77–78	Rejection
Cartoons 79–80	Delinquency

Antisocial behaviours

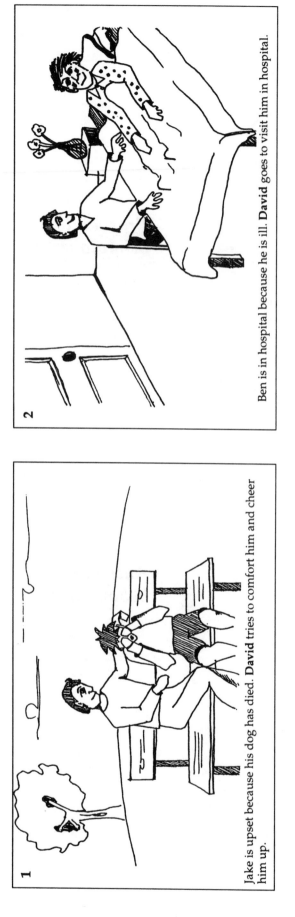

1

Jake is upset because his dog has died. **David** tries to comfort him and cheer him up.

3

David sees a group of children bullying Barney. He goes over and shouts "STOP".

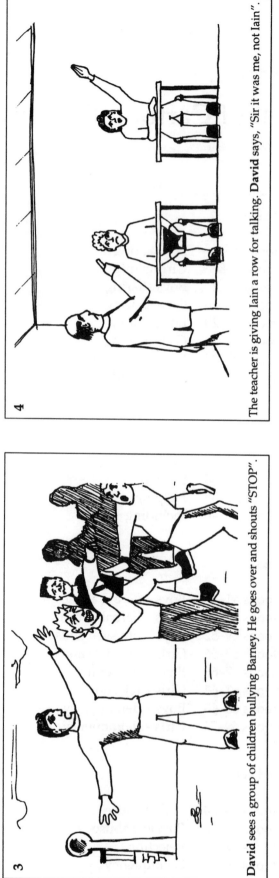

2

Ben is in hospital because he is ill. **David** goes to visit him in hospital.

4

The teacher is giving Iain a row for talking. **David** says, "Sir it was me, not Iain".

Cartoons 1–4   Boys caring

5

Ulla is upset because her dog has died. **Tina** tries to comfort her and cheer her up.

7

Tina sees a group of children bullying Maya. She goes over and shouts "STOP".

6

Shona is in hospital because she is ill. **Tina** goes to visit her in hospital.

8

The teacher is giving Amy a row for talking. Tina says, "Miss, it was me, not Amy".

Cartoons 5–8   Girls caring

Cartoons 9–12   Boys sharing

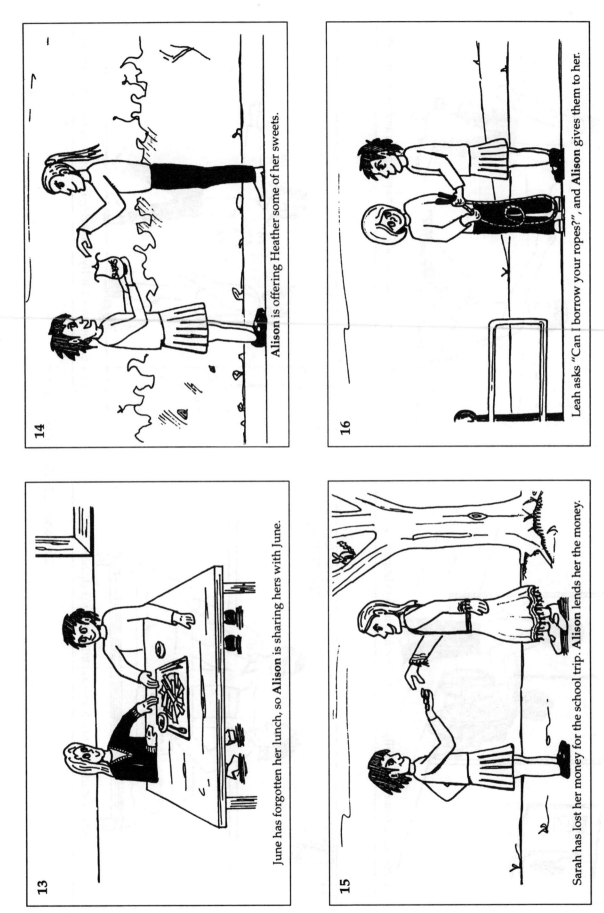

Cartoons 13–16   Girls sharing

17

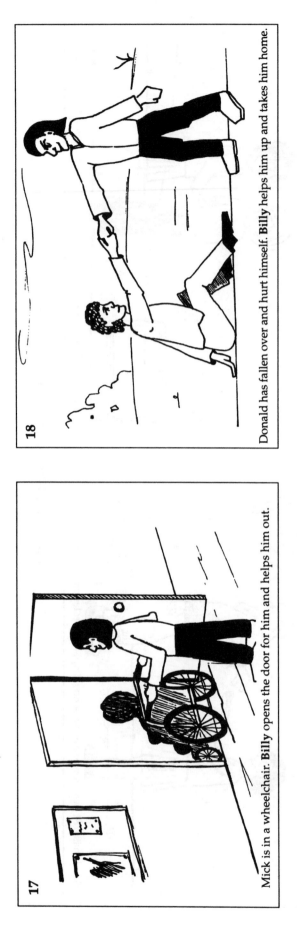

Mick is in a wheelchair. **Billy** opens the door for him and helps him out.

18

Donald has fallen over and hurt himself. **Billy** helps him up and takes him home.

19

Colin is stuck with his classwork. **Billy** tries to help him.

20

Todd is a new boy at school. **Billy** is showing him the way to the dinner hall.

Cartoons 17–20   Boys helping

21 Karen is in a wheelchair. **Katie** opens the door for her and helps her out.

22 Kath has fallen over and hurt herself. **Katie** helps her up and takes her home.

23 Nicola is stuck with her classwork. **Katie** tries to help her.

24 Emma is a new girl at school. **Katie** is showing her the way to the dinner hall.

Cartoons 21–24   Girls helping

96

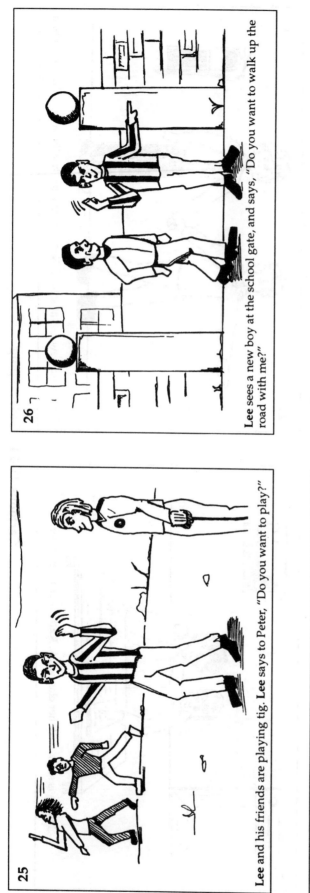

25 Lee and his friends are playing tig. **Lee** says to Peter, "Do you want to play?"

26 **Lee** sees a new boy at the school gate, and says, "Do you want to walk up the road with me?"

27 Simon is sitting alone in the dining hall. **Lee** asks, "Can I sit beside you?"

28 **Lee** asks Tim, "Do you want to come home to my house for tea?"

Cartoons 25–28 Boys including

30 Mia sees a new girl at the school gate and says, "Do you want to walk up the road with me?"

32 **Mia** asks Susan, "Do you want to come home to my house for tea?"

29 Mia and her friends are playing tig. **Mia** says to Beth, "Do you want to play?"

31 Jill is sitting alone in the dining hall. **Mia** asks, "Can I sit beside you?"

Cartoons 29–32   Girls including

33

Tina is in hospital because she is ill. **David** goes to visit her in hospital.

34

David is in hospital because he is ill. **Tina** goes to visit him in hospital

Cartoons 33–34 Caring

35

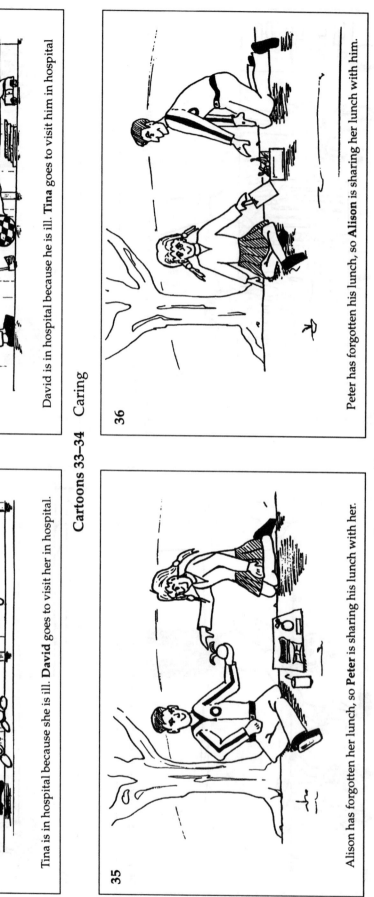

Alison has forgotten her lunch, so **Peter** is sharing his lunch with her.

36

Peter has forgotten his lunch, so **Alison** is sharing her lunch with him.

Cartoons 35–36 Sharing

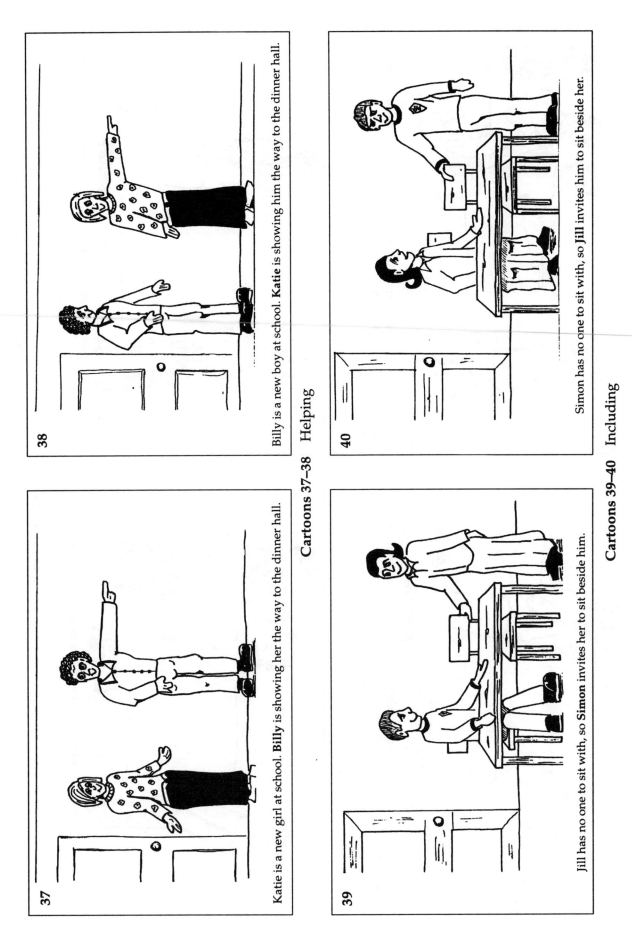

37 Katie is a new girl at school. **Billy** is showing her the way to the dinner hall.

38 Billy is a new boy at school. **Katie** is showing him the way to the dinner hall.

Cartoons 37–38 Helping

39 Jill has no one to sit with, so **Simon** invites her to sit beside him.

40 Simon has no one to sit with, so **Jill** invites him to sit beside her.

Cartoons 39–40 Including

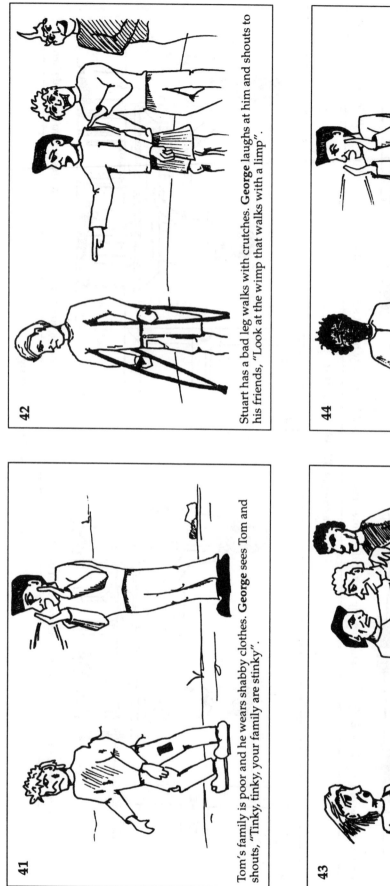

41

Tom's family is poor and he wears shabby clothes. **George** sees Tom and shouts, "Tinky, tinky, your family are stinky".

42

Stuart has a bad leg walks with crutches. **George** laughs at him and shouts to his friends, "Look at the wimp that walks with a limp".

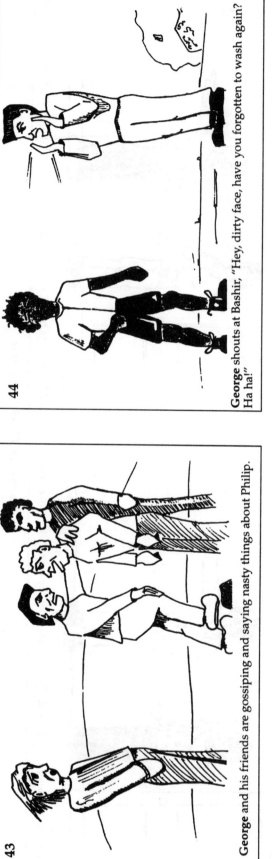

43

George and his friends are gossiping and saying nasty things about Philip.

44

George shouts at Bashir, "Hey, dirty face, have you forgotten to wash again? Ha ha!"

Cartoons 41–44   Boys – verbal abuse

46

Ann has a bad leg and walks with crutches. **Jane** laughs at her and shouts to her friends, "Look at wimp that walks with a limp".

48

Jane shouts at Nomita, "Hey dirty face, have you forgotten to wash again?".

45

Margaret's family is poor. **Jane** sees Margaret and shouts, Tinky, tinky, your family are stinky."

47

Jane and her friends are gossiping and saying nasty things about Helen.

Cartoons 45–48 Girls – verbal abuse

49

Keith is looking at books in the school library. Michael spits at him.

50

Michael sees Kevin in the street and throws a stone at him.

51

Michael kicks Jon and makes him drop his drink.

52

Michael and his pals are bullying Lenny after school.

Cartoons 49–52   Boys – physical abuse

102

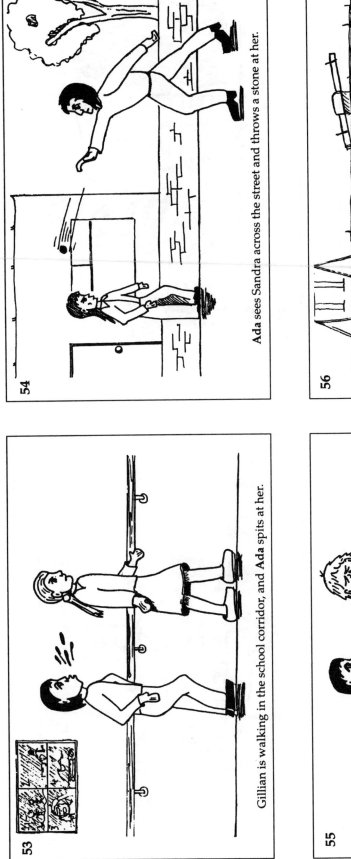

53

Gillian is walking in the school corridor, and Ada spits at her.

54

Ada sees Sandra across the street and throws a stone at her.

55

Ada doesn't like Penny, so she goes and kicks her.

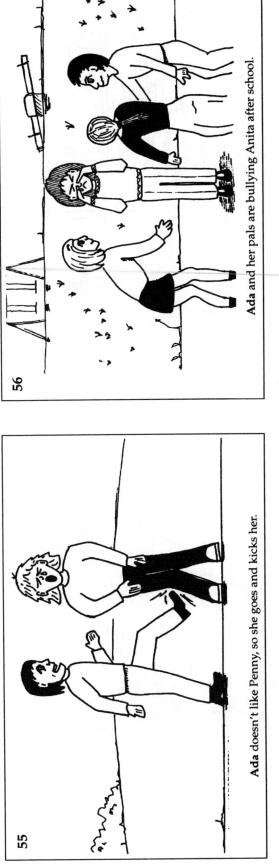

56

Ada and her pals are bullying Anita after school.

Cartoons 53–56   Girls – physical abuse

103

57 Jim and **Ben** are working beside each other in class. Jim asks Ben what to do, but **Ben** won't help him.

58 Jack wants **Ben** to sit beside him, but **Ben** ignores him and sits with someone else.

59 **Ben** and his pals are going to the park to play football. **Ben** tells Brian that he can't come with them.

60 **Ben** and his pals see Ossie coming. They run and hide behind behind the wall so that they don't have to play with him.

Cartoons 57–60   Boys – rejection

61

Carol and **Rachel** are working beside each other in class. Carol asks Rachel what to do, but **Rachel** won't tell her.

62

Jackie wants **Rachel** to sit beside her, but **Rachel** ignores her, and sits with someone else.

63

Rachel and her pals are going to play in the park. **Rachel** tells Jinny that she can't play with them.

64

Rachel and her pals see Susie coming. They run and hide behind the wall, so they don't have to play with her.

Cartoons 61–64   Girls – rejection

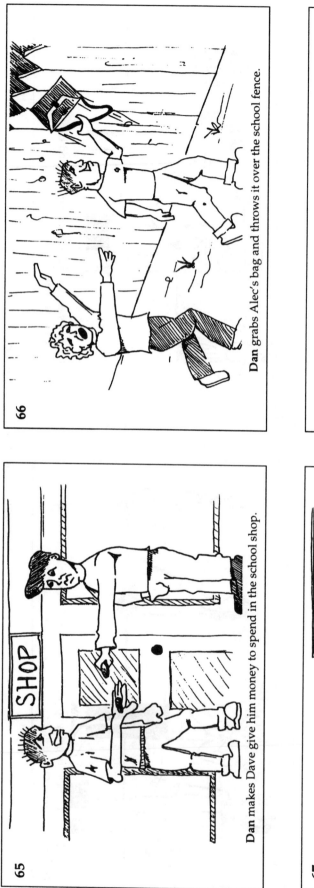

Dan grabs Alec's bag and throws it over the school fence.

66

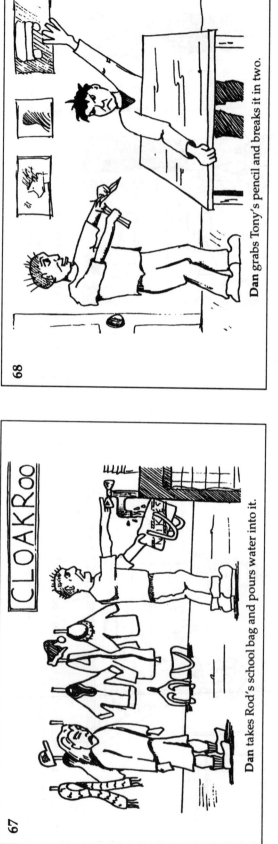

Dan grabs Tony's pencil and breaks it in two.

68

Dan makes Dave give him money to spend in the school shop.

65

Dan takes Rod's school bag and pours water into it.

67

Cartoons 65–68   Boys – delinquency

70

Nina grabs Cassie's bag from her, and throws it over the school fence.

69

Nina makes Tracey give her money to spend in the school shop.

72

Nina takes Lisa's pencil and breaks it in two.

71

Nina takes Paula's bag and pours water into it.

Cartoons 69–72   Girls – delinquency

107

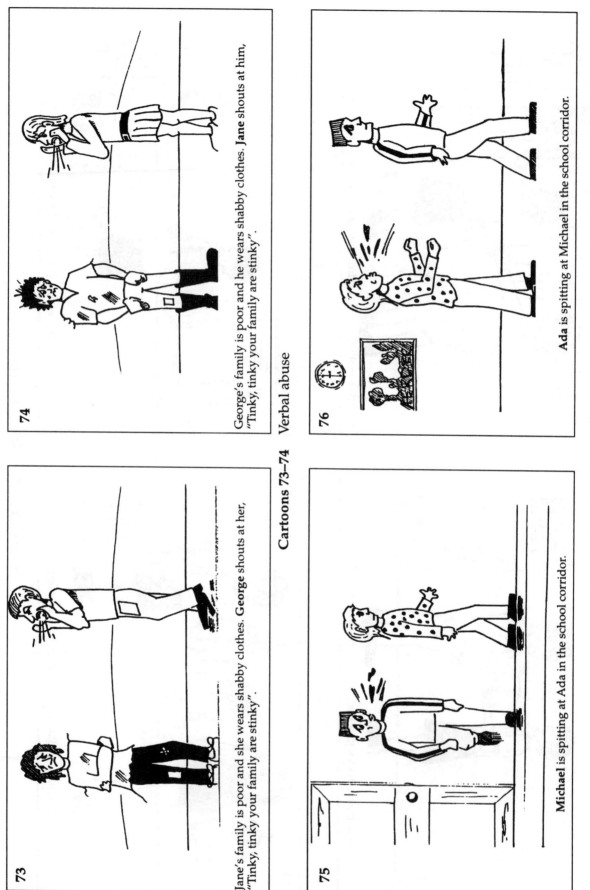

73

Jane's family is poor and she wears shabby clothes. **George** shouts at her,
"Tinky, tinky your family are stinky".

74

George's family is poor and he wears shabby clothes. **Jane** shouts at him,
"Tinky, tinky your family are stinky".

Cartoons 73–74 Verbal abuse

75

Michael is spitting at Ada in the school corridor.

76

Ada is spitting at Michael in the school corridor.

Cartoons 75–76 Physical abuse

108

77 Ben and his pals are playing tig. **Ben** tells Rachel that she can't play with them.

78 Rachel and her pals are playing tig. **Rachel** tells Ben that he can't play with them.

Cartoons 77–78 Rejection

79 Dan makes Nina give him money to spend in the school shop.

80 Nina makes Dan give her money to spend in the school shop.

Cartoons 79–80 Delinquency

109

References

Adalbjarnardottir, S. (1994) 'Understanding children and ourselves: teachers' reflections on social development in the classroom', *Teaching and Teacher Education*, **10**, 409–21.

Advisory Centre for Education/Childline (1994) *Bullying: Advice for Parents (factsheet)*. London: Childline.

Barnett, M. (1987), 'Empathy and related responses in children', in Eisenberg, N. and Strayer, J. (eds) *Empathy and its development*.

Brock, E. (1992) *A Positive Approach to Bullying: A Workshop for Professionals*. London: Longman.

Childline (1994) See Advisory Centre for Education/Childline (1994).

Damon, W. (1977) *The Social World of the Child*. San Francisco: Jossey-Bass.

Damon, W. and Killen, M. (1982) 'Peer interaction and the process of change in children's moral reasoning', *Merrill Palmer Quarterly* **28**, 347–67.

Department for Education (1994) *Bullying: Don't Suffer In Silence: An Anti-bullying Pack For Schools*. London: HMSO.

Dunn, J. (1993) *Young Children's Close Relationships: Beyond Attachment*. Newbury Park: Sage.

Dunn, J. (ed.) (1995) *Connections Between Emotion and Understanding in Development*. Hove: Erlbaum.

Eisenberg, N. (1982) *The Development of Prosocial Behaviour*. New York: Academic Press.

Eisenberg, N. and Strayer, J. (1987) *Empathy and its development*. Cambridge: Cambridge University Press.

Eisenberg-berg, N. and Hand, M. (1979) 'The relationship of preschoolers' reasoning about prosocial moral conflicts to prosocial behaviour', *Child Development*, **50**, 356–63.

Elliott, M. and Kilpatrick, J. (1994) *How To Stop Bullying: A Kidscape Training Guide*. London: Kidscape.

Foot, H., Morgan, M. and Shute, R. (1990) *Children Helping Children*. Chichester: Wiley.

Gardner, H. (1983) *Frames of Mind: The Theory of Multiple Intelligences*. New York: Basic Books.

Garton, A. and Pratt, C. (1998) *Learning To Be Literate*. (2nd edition). Oxford: Blackwell.

Gilligan, C. (1982) *In a Different Voice: Psychological Theory and Women's Development*. Cambridge, Mass.: Harvard University Press.

Gulbenkian Foundation (1995) *Children and Violence: Report of the Commission on Children and Violence*. London: Calouste Gulbenkian Foundation.

Hoffman, M. (1987) 'The contribution of empathy to justice and moral judgment', in Eisenberg, N. and Strayer, J. (eds) *Empathy and its development*.

Housego, E. and Burns, C. (1994) 'Are you sitting too comfortably? a critical look at "circle time" in primary classrooms', *English in Education*, **28**, 23–29.

Johnstone, M., Munn, P. and Edwards, L. (1991) *Action against Bullying*. Edinburgh: Scottish Council for Research in Education.

Kidscape (1994) See Elliott, M. and Kilpatrick, J. (1994)

Kohlberg, L. (1976) 'Moral stages and moralisation: the cognitive developmental approach', in Lickona, T. (ed.) *Moral development and behaviour*. New York: Holt, Rinehart & Winston.

Kruger, A. and Tomasello, M. (1986) 'Transactive discussions with peers and adults', *Developmental Psychology*, 681–85.

Lansdown, G. (1996) 'The United Nations Convention on the Rights of the Child – Progress in the UK', in Nutbrown, C. (ed.) *Children's Rights and Early Education*. London: Chapman.

McLean, A. (1991) *Promoting Positive Behaviour in the Primary School*. Glasgow: Strathclyde Regional Council.

McLean, A. (1994) *Promoting Positive Relationships: Bullyproofing your School*. Glasgow: Strathclyde Regional Council.

Mair, C. and MacDonald, M. (1993) *The 'Friends Against Bullying' Approach*. Hermitage Academy, Helensburgh.

Marantz, M. (1988) 'Fostering prosocial behaviour in the early childhood classroom: review of the research', *Journal of Moral Education*, **17**, 27–39.

Mosely, J. (1996) *Quality Circle Time in the Primary Classroom*. Wisbech: L.D.A.

National Curriculum Council (1990a) *Curriculum Guidance 3: The Whole Curriculum*. York: National Curriculum Council.

National Curriculum Council (1990b) *Curriculum Guidance 8: Education for Citizenship*. York: National Curriculum Council.

National Curriculum Council (1993) *Spiritual and Moral Education: A Discussion Paper*. York: National Curriculum Council.

Olweus, D. (1993) *Bullying at School: What We Know and What We Can Do*. Oxford: Blackwell.

Piaget, J. (1932/77) *The moral judgement of the child*. Harmondsworth: Penguin.

Powney, J., Cullen, M., Schlapp, U., Glissov, P., Johnstone, M., Munn, P. (1995) *Understanding Values Education in the Primary School*. Edinburgh: SCRE.

Riccio, L. L. and Gordon, T. (1996) *An holistic view of the curriculum: empowering children to infuse the arts into their classroom, school, and community*. Paper presented at the Scottish Educational Research Association Conference, University of Dundee.

Ross, R. (1996) 'Pupil council creates partnership in learning', *Times Educational Supplement Scotland*, **8** November 1996, p. 6.

Rowe, D. and Newton, J. (1994) (eds) *You, Me, Us! Social and Moral Responsibility for Primary Schools*. London: Home Office.

Scottish Consultative Council on the Curriculum (1991) *Values in Education: An SCCC Paper for Discussion and Development*. Edinburgh: SCCC.

Scottish Consultative Council on the Curriculum (1995) *The Heart of the Matter: Education for Personal and Social Development*. Dundee: SCCC.

Scottish Office Education Department (1993) *National Guidelines: Personal and Social Development 5–14*. Edinburgh: SOED.

Selman, R. (1980) *The Growth of Interpersonal Understanding*. London: Academic Press.

Sharp, S. and Smith, P. K. (1994) *Tackling Bullying in your School: A Practical Handbook for Teachers*. London: Routledge.

Smith, P. K. and Cowie, H. (1991) *Understanding Children's Development.* Oxford: Blackwell.

Smith, P. K. and Sharp, S. (1994) *School Bullying: Insights and Perspectives.* London: Routledge.

Smith, P. K. and Thompson, D. (eds) (1991) *Practical Approaches to Bullying.* London: David Fulton.

Tahir, T. (1996) 'Citizen awards for PSE', *Times Educational Supplement Scotland,* 25 October 1996.

Tattum, D. P. and Tattum, E. (1992) *Social Education and Personal Development.* London: David Fulton.

Thompson, D. (1995) *Two years on: problems in monitoring anti-bullying policies in schools and their effect on the incidence of bullying.* Paper presented at the BERA/EERA European Conference on Educational Research, University of Bath.

Thompson, D., Whitney, I. Smith, P. K. (1994) 'Bullying of children with special needs in mainstream schools', *Support for Learning,* **9**, 103–6.

Topping, K. (1988) *The Peer-tutoring Handbook: Promoting Cooperative Learning.* London: Croom Helm.

Warnock, M. (1992) *The Uses of Philosophy.* Oxford: Blackwell.

Wheldall, K. and Merrett, F. (1984) *Positive Teaching.* London: Unwin.

White, M. (1990) 'Circle time', *Cambridge Journal of Education,* **20**, 53–6.

Whitney, I., Nabuzoka, D. Smith, P. K. (1992) 'Bullying in schools: mainstream and special needs', *Support for Learning,* **7**, 3–7.

Whitney, I. and Smith, P. K. (1993) 'A survey of the nature and extent of bullying in junior/middle and secondary schools', *Educational Research,* **35**, 3–26.

Subject Index

Author Index